THE
STORM:
OR, A
COLLECTION
of the Most Remarkable
CASUALTIES
AND
DISASTERS
which Happened in the Late
Dreadful TEMPEST,
BOTH BY
SEA AND LAND
by Daniel Defoe

The Lord hath his way in Whirlwind, and in the Storm, and the Clouds are the dust of his Feet. Nah. I. 3.

London
Spradabach Publishing
2025

Spradabach Publishing
BM Box Spradabach
London WC1N 3XX

*The Storm: Or, a Collection of the Most Remarkable
Casualties and Disasters which Happen'd in the Late
Dreadful Tempest, both by Sea and Land*

First published in 1704

First Spradabach edition published 2025
© Spradabach Publishing 2025

Interior design by Alex Kurtagic

ISBN 978-1-909606-57-9

British Library Cataloguing-in-Publication Data:
A catalogue record for this book is available from the British Library.

Table of Contents

Note on This Edition

The present is volume is based on the second edition by G. Sawbridge printed in London in 1705, with reference also to the first edition, printed in 1704 for the same publisher.

The spelling, punctuation, capitalisation, and italics have been left as in the original, with all their inconsistencies. A number of words or names were blanked out in the original, and the blank spaces have been left in too. Extensive quotes, however, have been set as blockquotes, and chapters have been set so each begins on a new page.

Editorial footnotes have been added and identified as such.

A full index has been generated. The names of towns and villages in the latter appear in their modern spelling, and, where clarification was thought needed, a footnote has been added on the relevant page of the main text.

The Preface

Preaching of Sermons is Speaking to a few of mankind: Printing of Books is Talking to the whole World. The Parson Prescribes himself, and addresses to the particular Auditory with the Appellation of My Brethren; but he that Prints a Book, ought to Preface it with a *Noverint Universi*, Know all Men by these Presents.

The proper Inference drawn from this remarkable Observation, is, That tho' he that Preaches from the Pulpit ought to be careful of his Words, that nothing pass from him but with an especial Sanction of Truth; yet he that Prints and Publishes to all the World, has a tenfold Obligation.

The Sermon is a Sound as of Words spoken to the Ear, and prepar'd only for present Meditation, and extends no farther than the strength of memory can convey it; a Book Printed is a Record; remaining in every Man's Possession, always ready to renew its Acquaintance with his Memory, and always ready to be produc'd as an Authority or Voucher to any Reports he makes out of it, and conveys its Contents for Ages to come, to the Eternity of mortal Time, when the Author is forgotten in his Grave.

If a Sermon be ill grounded, if the Preacher imposes upon us, treasspasses on a few; but if a Book Printed obtrudes a Falshood, if a Man tells a Lye in Print, he abuses Mankind, and imposes upon the whole World, he causes our Child to tell Lyes after us, and their Children after them, to the End of the World.

This Observation I thought good to make by way of Preface, to let the World know, that when I go about a Work in which I must tell a great many Stories, which may in, their own nature seem incredieble, and in which I must expect a great part of Mankind will question the Sincerity of the Relator; I did not do it without a particular sence upon me of the proper Duty of an Historian, and the abundant Duty laid on him to be very wary what he conveys to Posterity.

I cannot be so ignorant of my own Intentions, as not to know, that in many Cases I shall act the Divine, and draw necessary practical inferences from the extraordinary Remarkables of this Book, and some Digressons which I hope may not be altogether useless in this Case.

And while I pretend to a thing so solemn, I cannot but premise I should stand convinced of a double Imposture, to forge a Story, and then preach Repentance to the Reader from a Crime greater to than that I would have him repent of: endeavouring by a Lye to correct the Reader's Vices, and sin against Truth to bring the Reader off from sinning against Sence.

Upon this score, tho' the Undertaking be very difficult among such an infinite variety of Circumstances, to keep exactly within the bounds of Truth; yet I have this positive Assurance with me, that in all the subsequent Relations if the least Mistake happen, it shall not be mine.

If I judge right, 'Tis the Duty of an Historian to set every thing in its own Light, ant to convey matter of fact upon its legitimate Authority, and no other: I mean thus, (for I wou'd be as explicit as I can) That where a Story is vouch'd to him with sufficient Authority, be ought to give the World the spectal Testimonial of its proper Voucher, or else he is not just to the Story: and where it comes without such sufficient Authority, be ought to say so; otherwise he is not just to himself. In the first Case he injures the History, by leaving it doubtful where it might be confirm'd past all manner of question; in the last he injures his own Reputation, by taking upon himself the Risque, in case it proves a Mistake, of having the World charge him with a Forgery. And indeed, I cannot but own 'tis just, that if I tell a Story in Print for a Truth which proves otherwise, unless I, at the same time, give proper Caution to the Reader, by owning the Uncertainty of my Knowledge in the matter of fact, 'tis I impose upon the World; my Relater is innocent, and the Lye is My Own.

I make all these preliminary Observations, partly to inform the Reader, that I have not undertaken this Work without the serious Consideration of what I owe to Truth, and to Posterity; nor without a Sence of the extraordinary Variety and Novelty of the Relation.

I am sensible, that the want of this Caution is the Foundation of that great Misfortune we have in matters of ancient History; in which the Impudence, the Ribaldry, the empty Flourishes, the little Regard to Truth, and the Fondness of telling a strange Story, has dwindled a great many valuable Pieces of ancient History into meer Romance.

How have the Lives of some of our most famous Men, nay the Actions of whole Ages, drowned in Fable? Not that there wanted Pen-men to write, but that ther Writings were continually mixt with such Rhodomontades of the Authors that Posterity rejected them as fabulous.

From hence it comes to pass that Matters of Fact are handed down to Posterity with so little Certainty, that nothing is to be depended upon; from hence the uncertain Account of Things and Actions

in the remoter Ages of the World, the confounding
the Genealogies as well as Atchievements of Belus,
Nimrod, and Nimrus, and their Successors, the
Histories and Originals of Saturn, Jupiter, and the
rest of the Celestial Rabble, who Mankind would
have been ashamd to have call'd Gods, had they
had the true Account of their dissolute, exorbitant,
and inhumane Lives.

From Men we may descend to Action: and this
prodigious Looseness of the Pen has confounded
History and Fable from the beginning of both. Thus
the great Flood in Deucalion's Time is made to pass
for the Universal Deluge: the Ingenuity of Deda-
lus, who by a Clue of Thread got out of the Egyp-
tian Maze, which was thought imposible, is grown
into a Fable of making himself a pair of Wings,
and flying through the Air:—the great Drought and
violent Heat of Summer, thought to be the Time
when the Great Famine was in Samaria, fabl'd by
the Poets and Historians into the Story of Phae-
ton borrowing the Chariot of the Sun, and giving
the Horses their Heads, they run so near the Earth
as burnt up all the nearest Parts, and Scorch'd the
Inhabitants, so that they have been black in those
Parts ever since.

These, and such like ridiculous Stuff, have
been the Effects of the Pageantry of Historians in
former Ages: and I might descend nearer home,
to the Legends of Fabulous History which have
swallow'd up the Actions of our ancient Predeces-
sors, King Arthur, the Gyant Gogmagog, and the

Britain, the Stories of St. George and the Dragon, Guy Earl of Warwick, Bevis of Southampton,[1] and the like.

I'll account for better Conduct in the ensuing History: and tho' some Things here related shall have equal Wonder due to them, Posterity shall not have equal Occasion to distrust the Verity of the Relation.

I confess here is room for abundance of Romance, because the Subject may be Safer extended than in any other case, no Story being capable to be crowded with such Circumstances, but Infinite Power, which is all along concern'd with us in every Relation, is suppos'd capable of making true.

Yet we shall no where so Trespass upon Fact, as to oblige Infinite Power to the shewing more Miracles than it intended.

It must be allow'd, That when Nature was put into so much Confusion, and the Surface of the Earth and Sea felt such extraordinary a Disorder, innumerable Accidents would fall out that till the like Occasion happen may never more be seen, and unless a like Occasion had happen'd could never before be heard of: wherefore the particular Circumstances being so wonderful, serve but to remember Posterity of the more wonderful Extreme, which was the immediate Cause.

The Uses and Application made from this Terrible Doctrine, I leave to the Men of the Pulpit; only

---

1   The name as it appears in Mediaeval sources is Bevis of Hampton. —Ed.

take the freedom to observe, that when Heaven it self lays down the Doctrine, all Men are summon'd to make Applications by themselves. The main Inference I shall pretend to make or at least venture the exposing to publick View, in this case, is, the strong Evidence God has been pleas'd to give in this terrible manner to his own Being, which Mankind began more than ever to affront and despise: And I cannot but have so much Charity for the worst of my Fellow-Creatures, that I believe no Man was so hard'ned against the Sence of his Maker, but he felt some Shocks of his wicked Confidence from the Convulsions of Nature at this time.

I cannot believe any Man so rooted in Atheistical Opinions, as not to find some Cause to doubt whether be was not in the Wrong, and a little to apprehend the Possibility of Supreme Being, when be felt the terrible Blasts of this Tempest. I cannot doubt but the Atheist's hard'ned Soul trembl'd a little as well as his House, and he felt some Nature asking him some little Questions; as these—Am not I mistaken? Certainly there is some such thing asa God—What can all this be? What is the Matter in the World?

Certainy Atheism is one of the most Irrational Principles in the World; there is something incongruous in it with the Test of Humane Policy, because there is a Risque in the Mistake one way, and none another. If the Christian is mistaken, and it should at last ape pear gee there is no Future State, God or Devil, Reward or Punishment, where is the Harm of it? All he has lost is, that he has practis'd a few needless Mortifications, and took the pains to live a little move like a Man than he wou'd have done. But if he Atheist is mistaken, be has brought all the Powers, whose Being he deny'd, upon his Back, has provok'd the Infinite in the highest manner and must at last sink under the Anger of him whose Nature be has always disown'd.

I would recommend this Thought to any Man to confider of, one Way he can loose nothing, the other he may be undone. Certainly a wise Man would never run such an unequal Risque: a Man cannot answer it to Common Arguments, the Law of Numbers, and the Rules of Proportion are against hark: No Gamester will set at such a Main; no Man will lay such a Wager, where he may lose, but cannot win.

There is another unhappy Misfortune in the Mistake too, that it can never be discover'd till 'tis too late to remedy. He that resolves to die an Atheist, Shuts the Door against being convinc'd in time.

> If it shou'd so fall out, as who can tell,
> But that there is a God, a Heaven, and Hell,
> Mankind had best consider well for Fear,
> 't should be too late when his Mistakes appear.

If should not pretend to set up for an Instructor in this Case, were not the. Inference so exceding just; who can but preach where there is such a Text? when God himself speak's his own Power, he expects we should draw just Inferences from it, both for our Selves and our Friends.

If one Man, in an Hundred Years, Shall arrive at a Conviction of the Being of his Maker 'tis very well worth my While to write it, and to bear the Character of an impertinent Fellow from all the rest.

I thought to make some Apology for the Meanness of Stile, and the Method, which may be a little unusual, of Printing Letters from the Country in their own Stile.

For the last I only leave this Short Reasen with the Reader, the Desire I had to keep close to the Truth, and band my Relation with the true Authorities from whence I receiv'd it, together with some Justice to the Gentlemen concern, who, especially in Cases of Delivevances, are willing to record the Testimonial of the Mercies they received, and to set their Hands to the humble Acknowledgment. The Plainness and Honesty of the Story will plead for the Meanness of the Stile in many of the Letters, and the Reader cannot want Eyes to see what sort of People some of them come from.

Others speak for themselves, and being writ by Men of Letters, as well as Men of Principles, I have not Arrogance enough to attempt a Correction either of the Sense or Stile; and if I had gone about it, should have injur'd both Author and Reader.

These come dressed in their own Words because I ought not, and those because I could not mend em. I am perswaded, they ave all dress'd in the desirable, though unfashionable Garb of Truth, and I doubt not but Posterity will vead them with Pleasure.

The Gentlemen, what have taken the Pains to collect and transmit the Particular Relations here made publick, I hope will have their End answered in this Essay, conveying hereby to the Ages to come the Memory of the dreadfulness and most universal Judgment that ever Almighty Power thought fit to bring upon this Part of the World.

And as this was the true Native and Original Design of the first Undertaking, abstracted from any Part of the Printer's Advantage, the Editor and Undertakers of this Work, having their Ends entirely answer'd, hereby give their humble Thanks to all those Gentlemen who have so far approud the Sincerity of their Design as to contribute their Trouble, and help forward by their just Observations, the otherwise very difficult Under-taking.

If Posterity will but make the desired Improvement both of the Collector's Pains, as well as the several Gentlemens Care in furnishing the Particulars, I dare fay they will all acknowledge their End fully answer'd, and none more readily than

The Ages Humble Servant.

Of the Natural Causes and Original of Winds

Though a System of Exhalation, Dilation, and Extension, things which the Ancients founded the Doctrine of Winds upon, be not my direct Business; yet it cannot but be needful to the present Design to Note, that the Difference in the Opinions of the Ancients, about the Nature and Original of Winds, is a Leading Step to one Assertion: which I have advanc'd in all that I have said with Relation to Winds, *viz.* That there seems to be more of God in the whole Appearance, than in any other Part of Operating Nature.

Nor do I think I need explain my self very far in this Notion: I allow the high Original of Nature to be the Great Author of all her Actings, and by the strict Rein of his Providence, is the Continual and Exact Guide of her Executive Power; but still 'tis plain that in Some of the Principal Parts of Nature she is Naked to our Eye, Things appear both in their' Causes and Consequences Demonstration gives its Assistance, and finishes, our further Enquities: for we never enquire after God in those Works of Nature which depending upon the Course of Things are plain and demonstrative; but where we find Nature defective in her Discovery, where we see Effects but cannot reach their Causes; there 'tis most just, and Nature her self seems to direct 'tis to it, to end the rational Enquiry, and resolve it into Speculation: Nature plainly refers us beyond her Self, to the Mighty Hand of Infinite Power, the Author of Nature, and Original of all Causes.

Among these Arcana of the Sovereign Oeconomy, the Winds are laid as far back as any. Those Ancient Men of Genius who rifled Nature by the Torch-Light of Reason even to her very Nudities, have been run a-ground in this unknown Channel; the Wind has blown out the Candle of Reason, and left them all in the Dark.

Aristotle, in his Problems, Sect. 23. calls the Wind *Aeris Impulsum*, *Seneca* says, *Ventus est Aer Fluens*. The *Stoicks* held it, *Motum aut Fluxionem Aeris*. Mr. *Hobs*, Air mov'd in a direct or undulating Motion. Fournier, *Le Vent et un Movement Agitation del Air Causi par des Exhalations et Vapours.* The Moderns, a Hot and Dry Exhalation repuls'd by Antiperistasis; *Des Cartes* defines it, *Venti Nihil sunt nisi Moti Dilati Vapores.*[1] And various other Opinions are very judiciously collected by the Learned Mr. *Bohun* in his Treatise of the Origin and Properties of Wind,[2] P. 7. and concludes, *'That no one Hypothesis, how Comprehen sive soever, has yet been able to resolve all the Incident Phenomena of Winds'.* Bohun, *Of Winds*, P. 9.

This is what I quote them for, and this is all my Argument demands; the deepest Search into the Region of Cause and Consequence, has found out just enough to leave the wisest Philosopher in the dark, to bewilder his Head, and drown his Understanding. You raise a Storm in Nature by the very Inquiry; and at aft, to be rid of you, she confesses the Truth, and tells you, *It is not in Me, you must go Home and ask my Father.*

Whether then it be the Motion of Air, and what that Air is, which as yet is undefin'd, whether it is a Dilation, a previous Contraction, and then violent Extension as in Gun-Powder, whether the Motion is Direct, Circular, or Oblique, whether it be an Exhalation repuls'd by the Middle Region,

---

1   Aristotle's defition: 'Impulse of the air'; Seneca's: 'wind is flowing air'; the Stoics': 'movement or flow of air'; Descartes': 'winds are nothing but moved and expanded vapours'. —Ed.

2   A *Discourse Concerning the Origine and Properties of Wind: With an Historicall Account of Hurricanes, and Other Tempestuous Winds* (Oxford: Tho. Bowman, 1671).

and the Antiperistasis of that Part of the Heavens which is set as a Wall of Brass to bind up the Atmosphere, and keep it within its proper Compass for the Functions of Respiration Condensing and Rarifying, without which Nature would be all in Confusion; whatever are their efficient Causes, 'tis not much to the immediate Design.

'Tis apparent, that God Almighty, whom the Philosophers care as little as possible to have any thing to do with, seems to have reserv'd this, as one of those Secrets in Nature which should more directly guide them to himself.

Not but that a Philosopher may be a Christian, and some of the best of the Latter have been the best of the Former, as Vossius, Mr. Boyle, Sir Walter Raleigh, Lord Verulam, Dr. Harvey, and others; and I wish I could say Mr. Hobbs, for 'twas Pity there should lie any just Exceptions to the Piety of a Man, who had so few to his General Knowledge, and an exalted Spirit in Philosophy.

When therefore I say the Philosophers do not care to concern God himself in the Search after Natural Knowledge; I mean, as it concerns Natural Knowledge, meerly as such; for 'tis a Natural Cause they seek, from a General Maxim, That all Nature has its Cause within itself: 'tis true, 'tis the Darkest Part of the Search, to trace the Chain backwards to begin at the Consequence, and from thence hunt Counter, as we may call it, to find out the Cause: 'twould be much easier if we could begin at the Cause, and trace it to all its Consequences.

I make no Question; the Search would be equally to the Advantage of Science, and the Improvement of the World; for without Doubt there are some Consequences of known Causes which are not yet discover'd, and I am as ready to believe there are yet in Nature some Terra Incognita both as to Cause and Consequence too.

In this Search after Causes, the Philosopher, tho' he may at the same Time be a very good Christian, cares not at all to meddle with his Maker: the Reason is plain; We may at any time resolve all things into Infinite Power, and we do allow that the Finger of Infinite is the First Mighty Cause of Nature her self; but the Treasury of Immediate Cause is generally committed to Nature; and if at: any Time we are driven to look beyond her, tis because we are out of the way: 'tis not because it is not in her, but because we cannot find it.

Two Men met in the Middle of a great Wood; One was searching for a Plant which grew in the Wood, the Other had lost himself in the Wood, and wanted to get out: The Latter rejoyc'd when thro' the Trees he saw the open Country; but the Other Man's Business was not to get out, but to find what he look'd for: yet this Man no more undervalued the Pleasantness of the Champion Country than the other.

Thus in Nature the Philosopher's Business is not to look through Nature, and come to the vast open Field of Infinite Powers his Business is in the Wood; there stows the Plant he looks for; and 'tis there he must find it. Philosophy's around if it is forc'd to any further Enquiry. The Christian begins just where the Philosopher ends; and when the Enquirer turns his Eyes up to Heaven, Farewel Philosopher; 'tis a Sign he can make nothing of it here.

David was a good Man, the Scripture gives him that Testimony; but I am of the Opinion, he was a better King than a Scholar, more a ascent than a Philosopher: and it seems very proper to judge that David was upon the Search of Natural Causes, and found himself puzzled as to the Enquiry, when he finishes the Enquiry with two pious Ejaculations, *When I view the Heavens the Works of thy Hands, the Moon and the Stars which thou hast made; then I say, what is Man!* David may very rationally be suppos'd to be searching the Causes, Motions, and Influences of Heavenly Bodies; and finding his Phylosophy a-ground, and the Discovery not to answer his Search, he turns it all to a pious Use, recognizes Infinite Power, and applies it to the Extasies and Raptures of his Soul, which were always employ'd in the Charm of exalted Praise.

Thus in another Place we find him dissecting the Womb of his Mother, and deep in the Study of Anatomy; is having, as it may be well supposed, no Help from *Johan Remelini,*[3] or of the Learned

---

3   Johan Remmelin (1583 - 1632), a German physician and anatomist. He is best known for his anatomical work *Catoptrum Microcosmicum* (1619), which featured detailed anatomical

Riolanus,[4] and other Anatomists, famous for the most exquisite Discovery of human Body, and all the Vessels of Life, with their proper Dimensions and Use, all *David* could say to the Matter was, *Good Man*, to look up to Heaven, and admire what he could not understand, *Psal. -- -- I was fearfully and wonderfully mode*, &c.

This is very Good, and well becomes a Pulpit; but what's all this to a Philosopher? 'Tis not enough for him to know that God has made the Heavens, the Moon, and the Stars, but must inform himself where he has plac'd them, and why there; and what their Business, what their Influences, their Functions, and the End of their Being. 'Tis not enough for an Anatomist to know that he is fearfully and wonderfully made in the lower-most Part of the Earth, but he must see those lowermost Parts; search into the Method Nature proceeds upon in the performing the Office appointed, must search the Steps she takes the Tools she works by; and in short, know all that the God of Nature has permitted to be capable of Demonstration.

And it seems a just Authority for our Search, that some things are so plac'd in Nature by a Chain

---

illustrations, including layered flaps that could be lifted to reveal different parts of the human body. His work was widely used for medical education in the 17th century. —Ed.

4 Jean Riolan the Younger (1580 - 1657), a prominent French anatomist and physician. He was a professor of anatomy and botany in Paris and wrote Encheiridium Anatomicum et Pathologicum (1648), which was an influential textbook on human anatomy. —Ed.

of Causes and Effects, that upon a diligent Search we may find one what we look for: To search after what God has in his Sovereignty thought fit to conceal, may be criminal, and doubtless is so; and the Fruitlesness of the Enquiry is generally Part of the Punishment to a vain Curiosity: but to search after what our Maker has not hid, only cover'd with a thin Veil of Natural Obscurity, and which upon our Search is plain to be read, seems to be justified by the very Nature of the thing, and the Posibility of the Demonstration is an Argument to prove the Lawfulness of the Enquiry.

The Design of this Digression, is, in short, That as where Nature is plain to be search'd into, and Demonstration easy, the Philosopher is allow'd to seek for it; so where God has, as it were, laid his Hand upon any Place, and Nature presents us with an universal Blank, we are therein led as naturally to recognize the Infinite Wisdom and Power of the God of Nature, as *David* was in the Texts before quoted.

And this is the Case here; the Winds are some of those Inscrutables of Nature, in which humane Search has not yet been able to arrive at any Demonstration.

> The Winds, *says the Learned Mr.* Bohun, are generated in the Intermediate Space between the Earth and the Clouds, either by Rarefaction or Repletion, and sometimes haply by pressure of Clouds, Elastical Virtue of the Air, &c. from the Earth or Seas, as by Submarine or Subterra-

neal Eruption or Descension or Resilition from
the middle Region.

All this, though no Man is more capable of the
Enquiry than this Gentleman, yet to the Demonstration of the thing, amounts to no more than
what we had before, and still leaves it as Abstruse
and Cloudy to our Understanding as ever.

Not but that I think my self bound in Duty to
Science in General, to pay a just Debt to the Ex-
cellency of Philosophical Study, in which I am a
meer Junior, and hardly any more than an Ad-
mirer; and therefore I can-not but allow that the
Demonstrations made of Rarefaction and Dilata-
tion are extraordinary; and that by Fire and Water Wind may be rais'd in a close Room, as the
Lord *Verulam* made Experiment in the Case of
his Feathers.

But that therefore all the Causes of Wind are
from the Influences of the Sun upon vaporous Matter first Exhal'd, which being Dilated are oblig'd to
possess themselves of more Space than before, and
consequently make the Particles fly before them;
this does not seem to be a sufficient Remonstra-
tion of Wind: for this, to my weak Apprehension,
would rather make a Blow like Gun-Powder than
a rushing forward; at best this is indeed a probable Conjecture, but admits not of Demonstration
equal to other Phænomena in Nature.

And this 1s all I am upon, *viz.* That this Case has
not equal Proofs of the Natural Causes of it that we

meet with in other Cases: The-Scripture seems to confirm this, when it says in one Place, *He holds the Wind in his Hand*; as if he should mean, Other things are left to the Common Discoveries of Natural Inquiry, but this is a thing he holds in his own Hand, and has conceal'd it from the Search of the most Diligent and Piercing Understanding: This is further confirm'd by the Wards of our Saviour, *The Wind blows where it lifteth, and thou hearest the Sound thereof, but knowest not whence it cometh*; 'tis plainly express'd to signify that the Causes of the Wind are not equally discover'd by Natural Enquiry as the rest of Nature is.

If I would carry this Matter on, and travel into the Seas, and Mountains of *America*, where the Mansones, the Trade-Winds, the Sea-Breezes, and such Winds as we have little Knowledge of, are more common; it would yet more plainly appear, *That me hear the Sound, but know not from whence they come.*

Nor is the Cause of their Motion parallel to the Surface of the Earth, a less Mystery than their real Original, or the Difficulty of their Generation: and though some People have been forward to prove the Gravity of the Particles must cause the Motion to be oblique; 'tis: plain it must be very little so, or else Navigation would be impracticable, and in extroardinary Cases where the Pressure above is perpendicular, it has been fatal to Ships, Houses, and would have terrible Effects in the World, if it should more frequently be so.

From this I draw only this Conclusion, That the Winds are a Part of the Works of God by Nature, in which he has been pleased to communicate less of Demonstration to us than in other Cases; that the Particulars more directly lead us to Speculations, and refer us to Infinite Power more than the other Parts of Nature does.

That the Wind is more expressive and adapted to his Immediate Power, as he is pleas'd to exert it in extraordinary Cases in the World.

That 'tis more frequently made use of as the Executioner of his Judgments in the World, and extraordinary Events are brought to pass by it.

From these three Heads we are brought down directly to speak of the Particular Storm before us; *viz.* The Greatest, the Longest in Duration, the widest in Extent, of all the Tempests and Storms that History gives any Account of since the Beginning of Time.

In the further Conduct of the Story, 'twill not be foreign to the Purpose, nor unprofitable to the Reader, to review the Histories of ancient Time and remote Countries, and examine in what Manner God has been pleas'd to execute his Judgments by Storms and Tempests; what kind of things they have been, and what the Consequences of them; and then bring down the Parallel tot he Dreadful Instance before us.

We read in the Scripture of Two Great Storms; One past, and the Other to come. Whether the last be not Allegorical rather than Prophetical, I shall not busie my self to determine.

The First was when God caused a strong Wind to blow upon the Face of the Delug'd World; to put a stop to the Flood, and reduce the Waters to their proper Channel.

I with our Naturalists would explain that. Wind to us, and tell us which way it blew, or how it is possible that any direct Wind could cause the Waters to ebb; for to me it seems, that the Deluge being universal, that Wind which blew the Waters from one Part must blow them up in another.

Whether it was not some perpendicular Gusts that might by their Force separate the Water and the Earth, and cause the Water driven from off the Land to *subside* by its own Pressure.

I shall dive no farther into that mysterious Deluge, which has some things in it which recommend the Story rather to our Faith than Demonstration.

The Other Storm I find in the Scripture is in the Psa. 11. 6. *God shall rain upon the Wicked, Plagues, Fire, and a horrible Tempest*. What this shall be, we wait to know; and happy are they who shall be secured from its Effects.

Histories are full of Instances of violent Tempests and Storms in sundry particular Places. What that was, which mingled with such violent Lightnings set the Cities of *Sodom* and *Gomorrah* on fire, remains to me yet undecided: nor am I satisfied the Effect it had on the Waters of the Lake, which are to this Day call'd the *Dead Sea*, are such as some fabulous Authors have related, and as Travellers take upon them to say.

Of the Opinion of the Ancients, that This Island was More Subject to Storms than Other Parts of the World

I am not of Opinion with the early Ages of the World, when these Islands were first known, that they were the most Terrible of any Part of the World for Storms and Tempests.

Cambden tells us, The *Britains* were distinguish'd from all the World by unpassable Seas and terrible Northern Winds, which made the *Albion* Shores dreadful to Sailors; and this part of the World was therefore reckoned the utmost Bounds of the Northern known Land, beyond which none had ever sailed: a quotes a great variety of ancient Authors this purpose; some of which I present as Specimen.

Et penitus toto divisos orbe Britannos,
Britain's disjoyn'd from all the well known World.[1]
Quam lĩtus adusta,
Horrescit Libya, ratibusque impervia[2] *Thule*
Ignotumque fretum.[3]

Claud.

And if the Notions the World then h were true, it would be very absurd for us who live here to pretend Miracles in any Extremes of Tempests; since by what the Poets of the Ages flourish'd about stormy Weather, was the native and most proper Epithet of the Place:

Belluosus gut remotis
Obstrepit Oceanus Britannis.

Hor.[4]

Nay, some are for placing the Nativity the Winds hereabouts, as if they had been all generated here, and the Confluence of Matter had made this Island its General Rendezvous.

But I shall easily show, that there are several Places in the World far better adapted be the Gen-

---

1   This is originally from Virgil's Georgics, Book 1, line 67. —Ed.

2   Taken frequenly for Britain.

3   'Whom sun-scorched Libya dreads, and Thule, inaccessible to ships, shudders at, and the unknown sea [lies between].' —Ed.

4   'The roaring, beastly Ocean
    resounds around the distant Britons.'

    The author misatributes these verses to Horace, but they are by Claudian, from *De Bello Gildonico.*

eral Receptacle or Centre of Vapours, to supply a Fund of Tempestuous: Matter, than *England*; as particularly the with Lakes of *North America*: Of which afterwards.

And yet I have two Notions, one real, one imaginary, of the Reasons which gave the Ancients such terrible Apprehensions of this Part of the World; which of late we find as Habitable and Navigable as any of the rest.

The real Occasion I suppose thus: That before the Multitude and Industry of Inhabitants prevail'd to the managing, enclosing, and improving the Country, the vast Tract of Land in this Island which continually lay open to the Flux of the Sea, and to the Inundations of Land-Waters, were as so many standing Lakes; from whence the Sun continually exhaling vast quantities of moist Vapours, the Air could not but be continually crowded with ail those Parts of necessary Matter to which we ascribe the Original of Winds, Rains, Storms, and the like.

He that is acquainted with the Situation of *England*, and can reflection the vast Quantities of flat Grounds, on the Banks of all our navigable Rivers, and the Shores of the Sea, which Lands at least lying under Water every Spring-Tide, and being thereby continually full of moisture, were like a stagnated standing body of Water brooding Vapours in the Interval of the Tide, must own that at least a fifteenth part of the whole Island may come into this Denomination.

Let him that doubts the Truth of this, examine a little the Particulars; let him stand upon *Shooters-Hill* in *Kent*, and view the Mouth of the River *Thames*, and consider what a River it must be when none of the Marshes on either side were wall'd in from the Sea, and when the Sea without all question flow'd up to the Foot of the Hills on either Shore, and up every Creek, where he must allow is now dry Land on either side the River for two Miles in breadth at least, sometimes three or four, for above forty Miles on both sides the River.

Let him farther reflect, how all these Parts lay when, as our ancient Histories relate, the *Danish* Fleet came up almost to *Hartford*; so that all that Range of fresh Marshes which reach for twenty five Miles in length, from Ware to the River *Thames*, must be a Sea.

In short, Let any such considering Person imagine the vast Tract of Marsh-Lands on both sides the River *Thames*, to *Harwich* on the *Essex* side, and to *Whitstable* on the *Kentish* side, the Levels of Marshes up the *Stour* from Sandwich to Canterbury, the whole Extent of Low-grounds commonly call'd *Rumney-Marsh*, from *Hythe* to *Winchelsea*, and up the Banks of the *Rother* all which put together, and being allow'd to be in one place cover'd with Water, what a Lake wou'd it be suppos'd to make? According to the nicest Calculations I can make, it cou'd not amount to less than 500000 Acres of Land.

The Isle of *Ely*, with the *Flats* up the several Rivers from *Yarmouth* to *Norwich*, *Beccles*, &c. the continu'd Les as in the several Counties of *Norfolk*, *Cambridge*, *Suffolk*, *Huntingdon*, *Northampton*, and *Lincoln*, I believe do really contain as much Land as the whole County of *Norfolk*; and 'tis not many Ages since these Countries were universally one vast Moras or Lough, and the few solid parts wholly unapproachable: insomuch that the Town of Ely it self was a Receptacle for the Male-contents of the Nation, where no reasonable Force cou'd come near to dislodge them.

'Tis needless to reckon up twelve or fourteen like Places in *England*, as the Moores in *Somerset-shire*, the Flat shores in *Lancashire*, *Yorkshire*, and *Durham*, the like in *Hampshire* and *Sussex*; and in short, on the Banks of every Navigable River.

The sum of the matter is this; That while this Nation was thus full of standing Lakes, stagnated Waters, and moist Places, the multitude of Exhalations must furnish the Air with a quantity of Matter for Showers and Storms infinitely more than it can be now supply'd withal, those vast Tracts of Land being now fenc'd off, laid dry, and turn'd into whol-some and profitable Provinces.

This seems demonstrated from *Ireland* where the multitude of Loughs, Lakes, Bogs, and moist Places, serve the Air with Exhalations, which give themselves back again in Showers, and make it be call'd, *The Piss-pot of the World*.

The imaginary Notion I have to advance on this Head, amounts only to a Reflection upon the Skill of those Ages in the Art of Navigation s which being far short of what it is since arrived to, made these vast Northern Seas too terrible for them to venture in: and accordingly, they rais'd those Apprehensions up to Fable, which began only in their want of Judgment.

The *Phœnicians*, who were our first Navigators, the *Genoese*, and after them the *Portuguese*, who arriv'd to extraordinary Proficiency in Sea Affairs, were yet all of them, *a we say*, Fair-weather Seamen: The chief of their Navigation was Coasting; and if they were driven out of their Knowledge, had work enough to find their way home, and sometimes never found it at all; but one Sea convey'd them directly into the last Ocean, from whence no Navigation cou'd return them.

When these, by Adventures, or Misadventures rather, had at any time extended their Voyaging as far as this Island, which, by the way, they always perform'd round the Coast of *Spain*, *Portugal*, and *France*, if ever such a Vessel return'd, if ever the bold Navigator arriv'd at home, he had done enough to talk on all his Days, and needed no other Diversion among his Neighbours, than to give an Account of the vast Seas mighty Rocks, deep Gulfs, and prodigious Storms he met with in these remote Parts of the known World: and this, magnified by the Poetical Arts of the Learned Men of those times, grew into a receiv'd Maxim of Navigation, That these Parts were so full of constant Tempests, Storms, and dangerous Seas, that 'twas present Death to come near them, and none but

Madmen and Desperadoes could have any Business there, since they were Places where Ships never came, and Navigation was not proper in the Place.

And *Thule*, where no Passage was
For Ships their Sails to bear.[5]

Horace has reference to this horrid Part of the World, as a Place full of terrible Monsters, and fit only for their Habitation, in the Words before quoted.

Belluosus que remotis
Obstrepit Oceanus Britannis.[6]

Juvenal follows his Steps;

Quanto Delpbino Balana Britannica major.[7]
Juv.

Such horrid Apprehensions those Ages had of these Parts, which by our Experience, and the Prodigy to which Navigation in particular, and Sciential Knowledge in general, is since grown, appear very ridiculous.

---

5   From Virgil's *Georgics*. —Ed.

6   Horace, *Odes* (Book 1, Ode 14).:

The noisy ocean, full of beasts,
Roars around the distant Britons. —Ed.

7   Juvenal, *Satires* (Satire 15, lines 72-73). —Ed.

For we find no Danger in our Shores, no uncertain wavering in our tides, no frightful Gulfs, no horrid Monsters, but what the bold Mariner has made familiar to him. The Gulfs which frighted those early Sons of *Neptune* are search'd out by our Seamen, and made useful Bays, Roads, and Harbours of Safety. The Promontories which running out into the Sea gave them terrible Apprehensions of Danger, are our Safety, and make the Sailors Hearts glad, as they are the first Lands they make when they are coming Home from a long Voyage, or as they are a good shelter when in a Storm our Ships get *under their Lee*.

Our Shores are founded, the Sands and Flats are discovered, which they knew little or no-thing of, and in which more real Danger lies, than in all the frightful Stories they told us; useful Sea-marks and Land-figures are plac'd on the Shore, Buoys on the Water, Light-houses on the highest Rocks; and all these dreadful Parts of the World are become the Seat of Trade, and the Centre of Navigation: Art has reconcil'd all the Difficulties, and Use made all the Horribles and Terribles of those Ages become as natural and familiar as Day-light.

The Hidden Sands, almost the only real Dread of a Sailor, and by which till the Channels between them were found out, our Eastern Coat must be really unpassable, now serve to make Harbours: and *Yarmouth* Road was made a safe Place for Shipping by them. Nay, when *Ports-*

mouth, Plymouth, and other good Harbours would not defend our Ships in the Violent Tempest we are treating of, here was the least Damage done of any Place in England, considering the Number of Ships which lay at Anchor, and the Openness of the Place.

So that upon the whole it seems plain to me, that all the dismal things the Ancients told us of Britain, and her terrible Shores, arose from the Infancy of Marine Knowledge, and the Weakness of the Sailor's Courage.

Not but that I readily allow we are more subject to bad Weather and hard Gales of Wind than the Coasts of *Spain, Italy,* and *Barbary:* But if this be allow'd, our lmprovement in the Art of Building Ships is so considerable, our Vessels are so prepar'd to ride out the most violent Storms, that the Fury of the Sea is the least thing our Sailors fear: Keep them but from a Lee Shore, or touching upon a Sand, they'll venture all the rest: and nothing is a greater satisfaction to them, if they have a Storm in view, than a found Bottom and good *Sea-room.*

From hence it comes to pass, that such Winds as in those Days wou'd have pass'd for Storms, are called only a *Fresh-gale,* or *Blowing hard.* If it blows enough to fright a South Country Sailor, we laugh at it: and if our Sailors bald Terms were set down in a Table of Degrees, it will explain what we mean.

Stark Calm.	*A Top-sail Gale.*
Calm Weather.	*Blows fresh.*
Little Wind.	*A hard Gale of Wind.*
A fine Breeze.	*A Fret of Wind.*
A small Gale.	*A Storm.*
A fresh Gale.	*A Tempest.*

Just half these Tarpawlin Articles, I presume, would have pass'd in those Days for a Storm; and that our Sailors call a Top-sail Gale would have drove the Navigators of those Ages into Harbours: when our Sailors reif a Top-sail, they would have handed all their Sails; and when we go under a main Course, they would have run *afore it* for Life to the next Port they could make: when our *Hard Gale* blows, they would. have cried a Tempest; and about the *Fret of Wind* they would be all at their Prayers.

And if we should reckon by this Account we are a stormy Country indeed, our Seas are no more Navigable now for such Sailors than they were then: If the, *Japoneses*, the *East Indians*, and such like Navigators, were to come with their thin Cockle-shell Barks and Calico Sails; if *Cleopatra's* Fleet, or *Cæsar's* great Ships with which, he fought the Battle of *Actium*, were to come upon our Seas, there hardly comes a *March* or a *September* in twenty Years but would blow them to Pieces, and then the poor Remnant that got, Home, would go and talk of a terrible Country where there's nothing but Storms and Tempests; when all the Matter is, the Weakness of their Shipping, and the Ignorance of their Sea-men: and I make no question but our Ships ride out many a worse Storm than that terrible Tempest which scatter'd *Julius Cæsar's* Fleet, or the same that drove *Æneas* on the Coast of *Carthage*.

And in more modern times we have a famous Instance in the *Spanish Armada*; which, after it was rather frighted than damag'd by Sir *Francis Drake's* Machines, not then known by the Name of Fireships, were scatter'd by a terrible Storm, and lost upon every Shore.

The Case is plain, 'Twas all owing to the Accident of Navigation: They had, no doubt, a hard Gale of Wind, and perhaps a Storm: but they were also on an Enemy's Coast, their Pilots out of their Knowledge, no Harbour to run into, and an Enemy a-stern, that when once they separated, Fear drove them from one Danger to another, and away they went to the North-ward, where they had nothing bue God's Mercy, and the Winds and Seas to help them. In all those Storms and Distreties which ruin'd that Fleet, we do not find an Account of the Loss of one Ship, either of the English or Dutch; the Queen's Fleet rode it out in the Downs, which all Men know is none of the best Roads in the World; and the Dutch rode among the Flats of the Flemish Coast, while the vast Galleons, not so well fitted for the Weather, were forced to keep the Sea, and were driven to and fro till they had got out

of their Knowledge; and like Men desperate, em-
brac'd every Danger they came near.

This long Digression I could not but think needful, in order to clear up the Case, having never met
with any thing on this Head before: At the same
time 'tis allow'd, and Histories are full of the Particulars, that we have often very high Winds, and
sometimes violent Tempests in these Northen
Parts of the World; but I am still of opinion, such
a Tempest never happen'd before as that which is
the Subject of these Sheets: and I refer the Reader
to the Particulars.

Of the Storm in General

Before we come to examine the Damage suffered by this terrible Night, and give a particular Relation of its dismal Effects; 'tis necessary to give a summary Account of the thing it self, with all its affrightning Circumstances.

It had blown exceeding hard, as I have already observ'd, for about fourteen Days past; and that so hard, that we thought it terrible Weather: Several Stacks of Chimnies were blown down, and several Ships were lost, and the Tiles in many Places were blown off from the Houses; and the nearer it came to the fatal 26th of *November*, the Tempestuouness of the Weather encreas'd.

On the *Wednesday* Morning before, being the 24th of *November*, it was fair Weather, and blew hard; but not so as to give any Apprehensions, till about 4 a Clock in the Afternoon the Wind encreased, and with Squauls of Rain and terrible Gusts blew very furiously.

The Collector of these Sheets narrowly escap'd the Mischief of a Part of a House, which fell on the Evening of that Day by the Violence of the Wind; and abundance of Tiles were blown off the Houses that Night: the Wind continued with unusual Violence all the next Day and Night; and had not the Great Storm follow'd so soon, this had pass'd for a great Wind.

On *Friday* Morning it continued to blow exceeding hard, but not so as that it gave any Apprehensions of Danger within Doors; to-wards Night it encreased: and about 10 a Clock, our Barometers inform'd us that the Night would be very tempestuous; the *Mercury* sank lower than ever I had observ'd it on any Occasion whatsoever, which made me suppose the Tube had been handled and disturb'd by the Children.

But as my Observations of this Nature are not regular enough to supply the Reader with a full Information, the Disorders of that dreadful Night having found me other Imployment, expecting every Moment when the House I was in would bury us all in its own Ruins; I have therefore subjoin'd a Letter from an Ingenious Gentleman on this very Head, directed to the *Royal Society*, and printed in the *Philosophical Transations*, No. 289. P. 1530. as follows.

A *Letter from the Reverend Mr.* William Derham, *F. R. S. Containing his Observations concerning the late Storm.*

S I R,

ccording to my Promise at the general Meeting of the R. S. on St. *Andrews* Day, I here send you inclos'd the Account of my Ingenious and Inquisitive Friend *Richard Townely*, Esq; concerning the State of the Atmosphere in that Part of *Lancashire* where he liveth, in the late dismal Storm. And I hope it will not be unacccepable, to accompany his with my own Observations at *Upminster*; especially since I shall not weary you with a long History of the Devastations, &c. but rather some Particulars of a more Philosophical Consideration.

And first, I do not think it improper to look back to the preceding Seasons of the Year. I scarce believe I shall go out of the way, to reflect as far back as *April, May, June* and *July*; because all these were wet Months in our Southern Parts. In *April* there fell 12,49 *l.* of Rain through my Tunnel: And about 6, 7, 8, or 9, *l.* esteem a moderate quantity for *Upminster. In May there fell more than in any Month of any Year since the Year* 1696, viz. 20,77 *l. June* likewise was a dripping Month, in which fell

14,55 *l.* And *July*, although it had considerable Intermissions, yet had 14,19 *l.* above 11 *l.* of which fell on *July* 28th and 29th in violent Showers. And I remember the News Papers gave Accounts of great Rains that Month from divers Places of *Europe*; but the *North of England* (which also escaped the Violence of the late Storm) was not so remarkably wet in any of those Months; at least not in that great proportion more than we, as usually they are; as I guess from the Fables of Rain, with which Mr. *Towneley* hath favoured me. Particularly *July* was a dry Month with them, there being no more than 3,65 *l.* of Rain fell through Mr. *Towneley*'s Funnel of the same Diameter with mine.

From these Months let us pass to *September*, and that we shall find to have been a wet Month, especially the latter part of it; there fell of Rain in that Month, 14,86 *l.*

October and *November* last, although not remarkably wet, yet have been open warm Months for the most part. My Thermometer (whose freezing Point is about 84) hath been very seldom below too all this Winter, and especially in *November*.

Thus I have laid before you as short Account as I could of the preceding Disposition of the Year, particularly as to wet and warmth, because I am of opinion that these had a great Influence in the late Storm; not only in causing a Repletion of Vapours in the Atmophere, but also in raising such Nitrosulphureous or other heterogeneous matter, which when mix'd together might make a sort of Explosion (like fired Gun-powder) in the Atmosphere. And from this Explosion I judge those Corruscations or Flashes in the Storm to have proceeded, which most People as well as my self observed, and which some took for Lightning. But these things I leave to better Judgments, such as that very ingenious Member of our Society, who hath undertaken the Province of the late Tempest; to whom, if you please, you may impart these Papers; Mr. *Halley* you know I mean.

From Preliminaries it is time to proceed nearer to the Tempest it self. And the foregoing Day, *viz. Thursday*, Nov. 25. I think deserveth regard. In the Morning of that day was a little Rain, the Winds high in the Afternoon S.b.E. and S. In the Evening there was Lightning; and between 9 and to of the Clock at Night, a violent, but short Storm of Wind, and much Rain at *Upminster*; and of Hail in some other Places,which did some Damage: There fell in that Storm 1,65 *l.* of Rain. The next Morning, which was *Friday, Novem.* 26. the Wind was S. S. W. and high all Day, and so continued till I was in Bed and asleep. About 12 that Night, the Storm awaken'd me, which gradually encreas'd till near 3 that Morning; and from thence till near 7 it continued in the greatest excess: and then began flowly to abate, and the *Mercury*[1] to rise swiftly. The Barometer I found at 12 h. ½ P. M, at 28,72,

---

1   A reference to the barometer, which at the time, operated with mercury and measured the pressure in inches, a level of 30 being considered normal. —Ed.

where it continued till about 6 the next Morning, or 6 ¼, and then hastily rose; so that it was gotten to 82 about 8 of the Clock, as in the Table.

How the Wind sat during the late Storm I cannot positively say, it being excessively dark all the while, and my Vane blown down also, when I could have seen: But by Information from Millers, and others that were forc'd to venture abroad; and by my own guess, I imagin it to have blown about S. W. by S. or nearer to the S. in the beginning, and to veer about towards the West towards the End of the Storm, as far as W. S. W.

The degrees of the Wind's Strength being not measurable (that I know of, though talk'd of) but by guess, I thus determine, with respect to other Storms. On *Feb.* 7. 169⁸/9. was a terrible Storm that did much damage. This I number ro degrees; the Wind then W.N.W. *vid. Ph. Tr. No.* 262. Another remarkable Storm was *Feb.* 3. 170½. at which time was the greatest descent of the ♀[2] ever known: This I number 9 degrees. But this last of *November*, I number at least 15 degrees.

As to the *Stations* of the *Barometer*, you have Mr. *Towneley*'s and mine in the following Table to be seen at one View.

As to *November* 17th (whereon Mr. *Towneley* mentions a violent Storm in *Oxfordshire*) it was a Stormy Afternoon here at *Upminster*, accompanied with Rain, but not violent, nor ♀ very low. *November* 11th and 12th had both higher Winds

---

2   Of the mercury, meaning the barometer. —Ed.

and more Rain; and the ♀ was those Days lower than even in the last Storm of *November* 26th. Thus, Sir, I have given you the truest Account! can, of what thought most to deserve Observation, both before, and in the late Storm. I could have added some other particulars, but that I fear I have already made my Letter long, and am tedious. I shall therefore only add, that I have Accounts of the Violence of the Storm at *Norwich*, *Beccles*, *Sudbury*, *Colchester*, *Rochford*, and several other intermediate places; but I need not tell Particulars, because I question not but you have better Informations.

A Table shewing the Height of the *Mercury* in the Barometer, at *Townely* and *Upminster*, before, in, and after the Storm.					
Townely			*Upminster*		
Day	Hour	Height of ☀	Day	Hour	Height of ☀
Novr.	7	28 98	Novr.	8	29 50
25	3	64	25	12	39
	9 ½	61		9	14
26	7	80	26	8	33
	3	70		12	28
	9 ½	47		9	10
				12	28 72
27	7	50	27	7 ½	82
	3	81		12	29 31
	9 ½	95		9	42
28	7	29 34	28	8	65
	3	62		12	83
	9	84		9	30 07
29	7	88	29	8	25

Thus far Mr. Derham's Letter

It did not blow so hard till Twelve a Clock at Night, but that most Families went to Bed; though many of them not without some Concern at the terrible Wind, which then blew: But about One, or at least by Two a Clock, 'tis suppos'd, few People, that were capable of any Sense of Danger, were so hardy as to lie in Bed. And the Fury of the Tempest encreased to such a Degree, that as the Editor of this Account being in *London*, and conversing with the People the next Days, understood, most People expected the Fall of their Houses.

And yet in this general Apprehension, no body durst quit their tottering Habitations; for whatever the Danger was within doors, 'twas worse without; the Bricks, Tiles, and Stones, from the Tops of the Houses, flew with such force, and so thick in the Streets, that no one thought fit to venture out, tho' their Houses were near demolish'd within.

The Author of this Relation was in a well-built brick House in the skirts of the City; and a Stack of Chimneys falling in upon the next Houses, gave the House such a Shock, that they thought it was just coming down upon their Heads: but opening the Door to attempt an Escape into a Garden, the Danger was so apparent, that they all thought fit to surrender to the Disposal of Almighty Providence, and expect their Graves in the Ruins of the House, rather than to meet most certain Destruction in the open Garden: for unless they cou'd have gone above two hundred Yards from any Building, there had been no Security;. for the Force of the Wind blew the Tiles point-blank, tho' their weight inclines them downward: and in several very broad Streets, we saw the Windows broken by the flying of Tile-sherds from the other side: and where there was room for them to fly, the Author of this has seen Tiles blown from a House above thirty or forty Yards, and stuck from five to eight Inches into the solid Earth. Pieces of Timber, Iron, and Sheets of Lead, have from hither Buildings been blown much farthers as in the Particulars hereafter will appear.

It is the receiv'd Opinion of abundance of People, that they felt, during the impetuous fury of the Wind, several Movements of the Earth; and we have several Letters which affirm it: But as an Earthquake must have been so general, that every body must have discernd it; and as the People were in their Houses when they imagin'd they felt it, the Shaking and Terror of which might deceive their Imagination, and impose upon their Judgment; I shall not venture to affirm it was so: And being resolv'd to use so much Caution in this Relation as to transmit nothing to Posterity without authentick Vouchers, and such Testimony as no reasonable Man will dispute; so if any Relation come in our way, which may afford us a Probability, tho' it may be related for the sake of its Strangeness or Novelty, it shall nevertheless come in the Company of all its Uncertainties, and the Reader left to judge of its Truth: for this Account had not been undertaken, but with design to undeceive the World in false Relations, and to give an Account back'd with such Authorities, as that the Credit of it shou'd admit of no Disputes.

For this reason I cannot venture to affirm that there was any such thing as an Earth-quake; but the Concern and Consternation of all People was so great, that I cannot wonder at their imagining several things which were not, any more than their enlarging on things that were, since nothing is more frequent, than for Fear to double every Object, and impose upon the Understanding, strong Apprehensions being apt very often to perswade us of the Reality of such things which we have no other reasons to shew for the probability of, than what are grounded in those fears which prevail at that juncture.

Others thought they heard it thunder, 'Tis confess'd, the Wind by its unusual Violence made such a noise in the Air as had a resemblance to Thunder; and 'twas observ'd, the roaring had a Voice as much louder than usual, as the Fury of the Wind was greater than was ever known: the Noise had also something in it more formidable; it founded aloft, and roar'd not very much unlike remote Thunder.

And yet tho' I cannot remember to have heard it thunder, er that I saw any Lightning, or heard of any that did in or near *London*; yet in the Countries the Air was seen full of Meteors and vaporous Fires: and in some places both Thundrings and unusual Flashes of Lightning, to the great terror of the Inhabitants.

And yet I cannot but observe here, how fearless such People as are addicted to Wickedness, are both of God's Judgments and uncommon Prodigies; which is visible in this Particular That: a Gang of hardned Rogues assaulted a Family at *Poplar*, in the very Height of the Storm, broke into the House, and robb'd them: it is observable, that the People cryed Thieves, and after that cryed Fire, in hopes to raise the Neighbourhood, and to get some Assistance; but such is the Power of Self-Preservation, and such was the Fear, the Minds of the People were possess'd with, that no Body would venture out to the Assistance of the distressed Family, who were rifled and plundered in the middle of all the Extremity of the Tempest.

It would admit of a large Comment here, and perhaps not very unprofitable, to examine from what sad Defect in Principle it must be that Men can be so destitute of all manner of Regard to invisible and superior Power, to be acting one of the vilest Parts of a Villain, while infinite Power was threatning the whole World with Disolation, and Multitudes of People expected the Last-Day was at Hand.

Several Women in the City of London who were in Travail, or who fell into Travail by the Fright of the Storm, were oblig'd to run the risque of being delivered with such a Help as they had; and Midwives found their own Lives in such Danger, that few of then thought themselves oblig'd to shew any Concern for the Lives of others.

Fire was the only Mischief that did not happen to make the Night compleatly dreadful; and yet that was not so every where, for in *Norfolk* the Town of —— was almost ruin'd by a furious Fire, which burnt with such Vehemence, and was so fann'd by the Tempest, that the Inhabitants had no Power to concern themselves in the extinguishing it; the Wind blew the Flames, together with the Ruines, so about, that there was no standing near it; for if the People came to Windward they were in Danger to be blown into the Flames; and if to Leward the Flames were so blown up in their Faces, they could not bear to come near it.

If this Distaster had happen'd in *London*, it must have been very fatal; for as no regular Application could have been made for the extinguishing it, so the very People in Danger would have had no Opportunity to have sav'd their Goods, and hardly their Lives: for though a Man will run any Risque to avoid being burnt, yet it must have been next to a Miracle, if any Person so oblig'd to escape from the Flames had escap'd being knock'd on the Head in the Streets; for the Bricks and Tiles flew about like small Shot; and 'twas a miserable Sight, in the Morning after the Storm, to see the Streets covered with Tyle-sherds, and Heaps of Rubbish, from the Tops of the Houses, lying almost at every Door.

From Two of the Clock the Storm continued, and encreased till Five in the Morning; and from

Five, to half an Hour after Six, it blew with the greatest Violence: the Fury of it was so exceeding great for that particular Hour and half, that if it had not abated as it did, nothing could have stood its Violence much longer.

In this last Part of the Time the greatest Part of the Damage was done: Several Ships that rode it out till now, gave up all; for no Anchor could hold. Even the Ships in the River of *Thames* were all blown away from their Moorings, and from *Execution-Dock* to *Lime-House Hole* there was but four Ships that rid it out, the rest weredriven down into the Bite, asthe Sailors call it, from *Bell-Wharf* to *Lime-House*; where they were huddel'd together and drove on Shore, Heads and Sterns, one upon another, in such a manner, as any one would have thought it had been impossible: and the Damage done on that Account was incredible.

Together with the Violence of the Wind, the Darkness of the Night added to the Terror of it; and as it was just New Moon, the Spring Tides being then up at about Four a Clock, made the Vessels, which were a-float in the River, drive the farther up upon the Shore: of all which, in the Process of this Story, we shall find very strange Instances.

The Points from whence the Wind blew, are variously reported from various Hands: 'Tis certain, it blew all the Day before at S. W. and I thought it continued so till about Two a Clock; when, as near as I could judge by the Impressions it made on the House, for we durst not look out, it veer'd to the S.

S.W: then to the W. and about. Six a Clock to W. by N. and still the more Northward it shifted, the harder it blew, till it shifted again Southerly about Seven a Clock; and as it did so, it gradually abated.

About Eight a Clock in the Morning it ceased so much, that our Fears were also abated, and People began to peep out of Doors; but 'tis impossible to express the Concern that appear'd in every Place: the Distraction and Fury of the Night was visible in the Faces of the People, and every Body's first Work was to visit and enquire after Friends and Relations. The next Day or Two was almost entirely spent in the Curiosity of the People, in viewing the Havock the Storm had made, which was so universal in *London*, and especially in the Out-Parts, that nothing can be said sufficient to describe it.

Another unhappy Circumstance with which this Disaster was join'd, was a prodigious Tide, which happen'd the next Day but one, and was occasion'd by the Fury of the Winds; which is also a Demonstration, that the Winds veer'd for Part of the Time to the Northward: and as it is observable, and known by all that understand our Sea Affairs, that a North West Wind makes the Highest Tide, so this blowing to the Northward, and that with such unusual Violence, brought up the Sea raging in such a manner, that in some Parts of England 'twas incredible, the Water rising Six or Eight Foot higher than it was ever known to do in the Memory of Mans; by which Ships were sleeted up upon the firm Land several Rods off fram the Banks, and an incredible Number of Cattle and People drown'd; as in the Pursuit of this Story will appear.

It was a special Providence that so directed the Waters, that in the River of Thames, the Tide, though it rise higher than usual, yet it did not so prodigiously exceed; but the Height of them as it was, prov'd very prejudicial to abundance of People whose Sellers and Ware-houses were near the River; and had the Water risen a Foot higher, all the Marshes and Levels on both sides the River had been over-flowed, anda great part of the Cattle drowned.

Though the Storm abated with the rising of the Sun, it still blew exceeding hard; so hard, that no Boats durst stir out on the River, but on extraordinary Occasions: and about Three a Clock in the Afternoon, the next Day being Saturday, it increas'd again, and we were in a fresh Consternation, left it should return with the same Violence. At Four it blew an extreme Storm, with sudden Gusts as violent as any time of the Night; but as it came with a great black Cloud, and some Thunder, it brought a hasty Shower of Rain which allay'd the Storm: so that in a quarter of an Hour it went off, and only continued blowing as before.

This sort of Weather held all Sabbath-Day and Monday, till on Tuesday Afternoon it encreased again; and all Tuesday Night it blew with such Fury, that many Families were afraid to go to Bed: And had not the former terrible Night harden'd the People to all things less than it self, this Night would have pass'd for a Storm fit to have been noted in our Almanacks, Several Stacks of Chimneys that stood out the great Storm, were blown down in this; several Ships which escap'd in the great Storm, perish'd this Night; and several People who had repair'd their Houses, had them untiled again. Not but that I may allow those Chimneys that fell now might have been disabled before.

At this Rate it held blowing till Wednesday about One a Clock in the Afternoon, which was that Day Seven-night on which it began; so that it might be called ome continued Storm from Wednesday Noon to Wednesday Noon: in all which time, there was not one Interval of Time in which a Sailor would not have acknowledged it blew a Storm; and in that time two such terrible Nights as I have describ'd.

And this I particularly noted as to Time, Wednesday, Nov. the 24th was a calm fine Day as at that time of Year shall be seen; 'till above Four a Clock, when it began to be Cloudy, and the Wind rose of a sudden, and in half an Hours Time it blew a Storm. Weduesday, Dec. the 2d. it was very tempestuous all the Morning; at One a Clock the Wind abated, the Sky clear'd, and by Four a Clock there was not a Breath of Wind.

Thus ended the Greatest and the Longest Storm that ever the World saw. The Effects of this terrible Providence are the Subject of the ensuing Chapter; and I close this with a Pastoral Poem sent us among the Accounts of the Storm from a very ingenious Author, and desir'd to be publish'd in this Account.

A
PASTORAL,
Occasion'd by the
Late Violent Storm

Damon, Melibæus

Dam.   *alking alone by pleasant Isis side,*
Where the two Streams their
wanton course divide,
And gently forward in soft Murmurs glide;
Pensive and sad I Melibæus meet,
And thus the melancholy Shepherd greet.
  Kind Swain, what Cloud dares overcast your brow,
Bright as the Skies o're happy Nile till now!
Does Chloe prove unkind, or some new Fair?

  Mel. *No Damon, mine's a publick, nobler Care;*
Such in which you and all the World must share.

41

One Friend may mollifie another's Grief,
But publick Loss admits of no relief.

Dam. I guess your Cause: O you that use to sing
Of Beauty's Charms and the Delights of Springs;
Now change your Note, and let your Lute rehearse
The dismal Tale in melancholy Verse.

Mel. Prepare then, lovely Swain; prepare to
The worst Report that ever reach'd your Ear.
My Bower you know, hard by you shady Grove,
A fit Recess for Damon's pensive Love:
As there dissolv'd I in sweet Slumbers lay,
Tir'd with the Toils of the precedent Day,
The blust'ring Winds disturb my kind Repose, ⎫
Till frightned with the threatning Blasts, I rose. ⎬
But O, what havock did the Day disclose! ⎭
Those charming Willows which on Cherwel's banks
Flourish'd, and thriv'd, and grew in evener ranks
Than those which follow'd the Divine Command? ⎫
Of Orpheus Lyre; or sweet Amphion's Hand, ⎬
By hundreds fall, while hardly twenty stand. ⎭
The stately Oaks which reach d the azure Sky,
And hiss'd the very Clouds, now prostrate lie.
Long a huge Pine did with the Winds contend;
This way, and that, his reeling Trunk they bend,
Till forc'd at last to yield, with hideous Sound
He falls, and all the Country feels the Wound.
Nor was the God of Winds content with these;
Such humble Victims can't his Wrath appease:
The Rivers swell, not like the happy Nile,

To fatten, dew, and fructifie our Isle:
But like the Deluge, by great Jove design'd
To drown the Universe, and scourge Mankind.
In vain the frighted Catte! climb so high;
In vain for Refuge to the Hills they fly;
The Waters know no Limits but the Sky.
So now the bleating Flock exchange in vain,
For barren Clifts, their dewy fertil Plain:
In vain, their fatal Destiny to shun,
From Severn's Banks to higher Grounds they run:
*   Nor has the Navy better Quarter found;*
There we've receiv'd our worst, our deepest Wound.
The Billows swell, and haughty Neptune raves,
The Winds insulting o're th'impetuous Waves.
Thetis incens'd, rises with angry Frown,
And once more threatens all the World to drown;
And owns no Power, but England's and her own.
Yet the Eolian God dares went his Rages
And ev'n the Sovereign of the Seas encage.
What tho' the mighty Charles of Spain's on board,
The Winds obey none but their blust'ring Lord.
Some Ships were stranded, some by Surges rent,
Down with their Cargo to the bottom went.
Th' absorbent Ocean could desire no more;
So well regal'd he never was before.
The hungry Fish could hardly wait the day,
When the Sun's beams should chase the Storm away,
But quickly Seine with greedy Fams their Prey.

    Dam. *So the great Trojan, by the Hard of Fate,*
And haughty Power of angry Juno's Hate,

While with like aim he cross'd the Seas, was tost,
From Shore to Shore, from foreign Coast to Coast:
Yet safe at last his mighty Point he gain'd;
In charming promis d Peace and Splendor reign'd.

Mel. *So way Great Charles, whom equal Glo-*
ries move,
Like the great Dardan Prince successful prove
Like him, mith Honour may he mount the Throne,
And long enjoy a brighter destin'd Crown.

CHAPTER IV

Of the Extent of This Storm, and from What Parts It Was Suppos'd to Come; with Some Circumstances as to the Time of It

A s all our Histories are full of the Relations of Tempests and Storms which have happened in various Parts of the World, I hope it may not be improper that some of them have been thus observ'd with their remarkable Effects.

But as I have all along insisted, that no Storm since the Universal Deluge was like this, either in its Violence or its Duration, so I must also confirm it as to the particular of its prodigious Extent.

All the Storms and Tempests we have heard of in the World, have been Gusts or Squauls of Wind that have been carried on in their proper Channels, and have spent their Force in a shorter space.

We feel nothing here of the Hurricanes of Bar-badoes, the North-Wests of *New-England* and *Virginia*, the terrible Gusts of the *Levant*, or the frequent Tempests of the *North Cape*. When *Sir Francis Wheeler*'s Squadron perish'd at *Gibralter*, [1]when the City of *Straelsond* was almost ruin'd by a Storm, *England* felt it not, nor was the Air here disturb'd with the Motion. Even at home we have had Storms of violent Wind in one part of *England* which have not been felt in another. And if what I have been told has any truth in it, in St. *George*'s Channel there has frequently blown a Storm at Sea right up and down the Channel, which has been felt on neither Coast, tho' it is not above 20 Leagues from the *English* to the *Irish* Shore.

Sir *William Temple* gives us the Particulars of two terrible Storms in *Holland* while he was there; in one of which the great Cathedral Church at *Utrecht* was utterly destroy'd: and after that there was a Storm so violent in *Holland*, that 46 Vessels were cast away at the *Texel*, and almost all the Men drowned: and yet we felt none of these Storms here.[2]

---

1   When Admiral Sir Francis Wheeler was commanding opera-tions in the Mediterranean during the Nine Years' War (1688–1697), his fleet suffered a devastating loss in 1694 due to a vio-lent storm near Gibraltar. —Ed.

2   English diplomat and writer, Sir William Temple (1628 - 1699) tells of the tornado that struck Utrecht on 1 August 1674, caus-ing widespread destruction and demolishing the central nave of St Martin's Cathedral, which was at the time still unfinished and insufficiently supported. Though the structure later un-

And for this very reason I have reserv'd an Abridgment of these former Cases to this place; which as they are recited by Sir William Temple, I shall put them down in his own Words, being not capable to mend them, and not vain enough to pretend to it.

> I stay'd only a Night at *Antwerp*, which pass'd
> with so great Thunders and Lightnings, that I
> promis'd my self a very fair Day after it, to go
> back to *Rotterdam* in the States Yacht, that still
> attended me. The Morning prov'd so; but to-
> wards Evening the Sky grew foul, and the Sea-
> men presag'd ill Weather, and to resolved to
> lie at Anchor before *Berge ap Zoom*, the Wind
> being cross and little. When the Night was fall-
> en as black as ever I saw, it soon began to clear
> up, with the most violent Flashes of Lightning
> as well as Cracks of Thunder, that I believe
> have ever been heard in our Age and Climate.
> This continued all Night; and we felt such a
> fierce Heat from every great Flash of Lightning,
> that the Captain apprehended it would fire his
> Ship. But about 8 the next Morning the Wind
> changed, and came up with so strong a Gale,
> that we came to *Rotterdam* in about 4 Hours,
> and there found all Mouths full of the Mischiefs
> and Accidents that the last Night's Tempest
> had occasioned both among the Boats and the
> Houses, by the Thunder, Lightning, Hail, or
> Whirlwinds. But the Day after came Stories to

---

derwent some restoration in the 19th and 20th centuries, the
collapsed nave was never rebuilt. Texel was a critical Dutch
anchorage and naval hub; the storm is likely the one in 1686,
which caused a massively destructive sea flood. —Ed.

the *Hague* from all Parts, of such violent Effects as were almost incredible: At *Amsterdam* they were deplorable, many Trees torn up by the Roots, Ships sunk in the Harbour, and Boats in the Channels; Houses beaten down, and several People were snatch'd from the Ground as they walk'd the Streets, and thrown into the Canals. But all was silenc'd by the Relations from Utrech, where the Great and Ancient Cathedral was torn in pieces by the Violences of this Storm; and the vast Pillars of Stone that supported it, were wreathed like a twisted Club, having been so strongly compos'd and cimented, as rather to suffer such a Change of Figure than break in pieces, as other Parts of the Fabrick did; hardly any Church in the Town escap'd the Violence of this Storm; and very few Houses without the Marks of it; a were the Effects of it less astonishing by the Relations from *France* and *Brussels* where the Damages were infinite, as well from Whirlwinds, Thunder, Lightning, as from Hailstones of prodigious Bigness. This was in the Year 1674.

In *November*, 1675. happen'd a Storm at North-West, with a Spring-tide so violent, as gave apprehensions of some loss irrecover'ble to the Province of *Holland*, and by several breaches in the great Diques near *Enchusen*, and others between *Amsterdam* and *Harlem*, made way for such Inundations as had not been seen before by any man then alive, and fill'd the Country with many relations of most deplorable Events. But the incredible mn and unanimous Endeavours of the People upon such occasions, gave a stop to the Fury of that Ele-

ment, and made way for recovering next Year
all the Lands, though not the People, Cattel, and
Houses that had been lost.

Thus far Sir William Temple.

I am also credibly inform'd that the greatest
Storm that ever we had in *England* before, and
which was as universal here as this, did no Damage in *Holland* or *France*, comparable to this
Tempest: I mean the great Wind in 1661. An Abstract of which, as it was printed in *Mirabilis Annis;* an unknown, but unquestion'd Author, take as
follows, in his own Words.

A dreadful Storm of Wind, accompanied with Thunder, Lightning, Hail and Rain; together with the sad Effects of it in many Parts of the Nation.

pon the 18*th of February*, 1661. being
Tuesday, very early in the Morning, there
began a very great and dreadful Storm of
Wind (accompanied with Thunder, Lightning,
Hail, and Rain, which in may: Places were as fast
as Brine) which continued with a strange and unusual Violence till almost Night: the sad Effects
whereof throughout the Nation are so many, that
a very great Volume is not sufficient to contain
the Narrative of them. And indeed some of them
are so stupendous and amazing, that the Report
of them, though from never so authentick Hands,

will scarce gain Credit among any but those that have an affectionate Sense of the unlimited Power of the Almighty, knowing and believing that there is nothing too hard for Him to do.

Some few of which wonderful Effects we shall give a brief Account of, as we have received them from Persons of most unquestionable Credit in the several Parts of the Nation.

In the City of *London*, and in *Covent Garden* and other Parts about *London* and *Westminster*, five or six Persons were killed outright by the Fall of Houses and Chimneys; especially one Mr. *Luke Blith* an Attorney, that lived at or near *Stamford* in the County of *Lincoln*, was killed that Day by the fall of a Riding-House not far from *Pickadilla*: and there are some very remarkable Circumstances in this Man's Case, which do make his Death to appear at least like a most eminent Judgment and severe Stroak of the Lord's Hand upon him.

From other Parts likewise we have received certain Information, that divers Persons were killed by the Effects of this great Wind.

At *Chiltenham* in *Gloucestershire*, a Maid was killed by the Fall of a Tree, in or near the Church-Yard.

An honest Yeoman likewise of *Scaldwel* in *Northamptonshire*, being upon a Ladder to save his Hovel, was blown off, and fell upon a Plough, died outright, and never spoke Word more.

Also at *Tewksbury* in *Gloucestershire*, a Man was blown from an House, and broken to Pieces,

At *Elsbury* likewise in the same County, a Woman was killed by the Fall of Tiles or Bricks from an House.

And not far from the same Place, a Girl was killed by the Fall of a Tree.

Near *Northampton*, a Man was killed by the Fail of a great Barn.

Near *Colchester*, a Young-man was killed by the Fell of a Wind-mill.

Not far from *Ipswich* in *Suffolk*, a Man was killed by the Fall of a Barn.

And about two Miles from the said Town of *Ipswich*, a Man was killed by the Fall of a Tree.

At *Langton*, or near to it, in the County of Leicester, one Mr. *Roberts* had a Wind-mill blown down, in which were three Men; and by the Fall of it, one of them was killed outrighe, a second had his Back broken, and the other had his Arm or Leg struck off; and both of them (according to our best Information) are since dead.

Several other Instances there are of the like Nature; but it would be too tedious to mention them: Let these therefore suffice to stir us up to Repentance, *left we likewise perish*.

There are also many Effects of this Storm which are cof another Nature, whereof we shall give this following brief Account.

The Wind hath very much prejudiced many Churches in several Parts of the Nation.

At *Tewksbury* in *Gloucestershire*, it blew down a very fair Window belonging to the Church there, both the Glass, and the Stone-work also; the Doors likewise of that Church were blown open, much of the Lead torn up, and some Part of a fair Pinnacle thrown down.

Also at *Red-Marly* and *Newin*, not far from Tewksbury, their Churches are extreamly broken and shatterd, if not a considerable part of them blown down.

The like was done to most, if not all the Publick Meeting-places at *Gloucester* City. And it is-reported, that some Hundreds of Pounds will not suffice to repair the Damage done to the Cathedral at *Worcester*, especially in that Part that is over the Quire.

The like Fate happen'd to many more of them, as *Hereford*, and *Leighton Beau-desart* in *Bedfordshire*, and *Eaton-Soken* in the same County; where they had newly erected a very fair Cross of Stone, which the Wind blew down: and, as some of the Inhabitants did observe, that was the first Damage which that Town sustained by the Storm, though afterwards in other respects also they were in the same Condition with their Neighbours. The Steeples also, and other Parts of the Churches of *Shenley*, *Waddon*, and *Woolston* in the County of *Bucks*, have been very much rent and torn by the Wind. The Spire of *Finchinfield* Steeple in the County of *Essex*, was blown down, and it brake through the Body of the Church, and spoil'd many of the Pews; some Hundreds of Pounds will not repair that Loss. But that which is most remarkable of this kind, is, the Fall of that most famous Spire, or Pinnacle of the Tower-Church in *Ipswich*: it was blown down upon the Body ef the Church, and fell reversed, the sharp End of the Shaft striking through the Leads on the South-side of the Church, carried much of the Timber-work down before it into the Alley just behind the Pulpit, and took off one Side of the Sounding board over the Pulpit: it shattered many Pews: The Weather-Cock, and the Iron upon which it stood, broke off as it fell; but the narrowed Part of the Wood-work, upon which the Fane stood, fell into the Alley, broke quite through a Grave-stone, and ran shoring under two Coffins that had been placed there one on another; that Part of the Spire which was pluck'd up was about three Yards deep in the Earth, and it is believed some Part of it is yet behind the Ground: some Hundreds of Pounds will not make good the Detriment done to the Church by the Fall of this Pinnacle.

Very great Prejudice has been done to private Houses; many of them blown down, and others extreamly shattered and torn. It is thought that five thousand Pounds will not make good the Repairs at *Audley-End House*, which belongs to the Earl of *Suffolk*.[3] A good Part also of the Crown-Office in the *Temple* is blown down. The Instances of this kind are so many and so obvious, that it would needlesly take up too much time to give the Read-

---

3   At the time, James Howard, 3rd Earl of Suffolk (1620–1689).
     —Ed.

er an Account of the Collection of them; only there has been such a wonderful Destrution of Barns, that (looking so much like a Judgment from the Lord, who the last Year took away our Corn, and this our Barns) we cannot but give a short Account of some Part of that Intelligence which hath come to our Hands of that Nature.

A Gentleman, of good Account, in *Ipswich*, affirms, that in a few Miles riding that Day, there was eleven Barns and Out-houses blown down in the Road within his View; and with in a very few Miles of *Ipswich* round about, above thirty Barns, and many of them with Corn in them, were blown down. At *Southold* not far from the Place before mentioned, many new Houses and Barns (built since a late Fire that happened there) are blown down as also a Salt-house is destroyed there: and a thousand Pounds, as it is believed, will not make up that particular Loss.

From *Tewksbury* it is certified, that an incredible Number of Barns have been blown down in the small Towns and Villages thereabouts. At *Twyning*, at least eleven Barns are blown down. In *Ashchurch* Parish seven or eight. At *Lee*, five. At *Norton*, a very great Number, three whereof belonging to one Man. The great Abby-Barn also at *Tewksbury* is Blown down.

It is credibly reported, that within a very few Miles Circumference in *Worcestershire*, about arm hundred and forty Barns are blown down. At *Finchinfield* in *Essex*, which is but an ordinary Village, about sixteen Barns were blown down. Also at a Town called *Wilchamsted* is the County of Bedford (avery small Village) fifteen Barns at least are blown down. But especially the Parsonage Barns went to wrack in many Places throughout the Land: ina few Miles Compass in *Bedfordshire*, and so in *Northamptonshire*, and other Places, eight, ten, and twelve are blown down; and at Yielding Parsonage in the County of *Bedford* (out of which was thrust by Oppression and Violence the late Incumbent) all the Barns belonging to it are down. The Instances also of this kind are innumerable, which we shall therefore forbear to make further mention of.

We have also a large Account of the blowing down of a very great and considerable Number of Fruit-Trees, and other Trees in several Parts; we shall only pick out two or three Passages which are the most remarkable. In the Countries of *Gloucester*, *Hereford*, and *Worcester*, several Persons have lost whole Orchards of Fruit-trees; and many particular Mens Loss hath amounted to the Value of forty or fifty Pounds at the least, meerly by Destruction of their Fruit-Trees: and so in other Parts of *England* proportionably the like Damage hath been sustained in this Respect. And as for other Trees, there has been a great Destruction made of them in many Places by this Storm. Several were blown down at *Hampton-Court*. And three thousand brave Oaks at least, but in one principal Part of the Forest of *Dean*, belonging to his Majesty. In a little Grove at *Ipswich*, belonging to the Lord of *Hereford* (which together with the Spice of the Steeple before-mentioned, were the most considerable Ornaments of that Town) are blown down at least two hundred goodly Trees, one of which was an Ash, which had ten Load of Wood upon it there are now few Trees left there.

In *Bramton Bryan Park* in the County of *Hereford*, belonging to Sir *Edward Harly*, one of the late Knights of the Bath, above thirteen hundred tees are blown down, and above six hundred in *Hopton Park* not far from it: and thus it is proportionably in most Places where this Storm was felt, And the Truth is, the Damage which the People of this Nation have sustained upon all Accounts by this Storm, is not easily to be valued: some sober and discreet People, who have endeavoured to compute the Loss of the several Countries one with another, by the Destruction of Houses and Barns, the blowing away of Hovels and Ricks of Corn, the falling of Trees, &c. do believe it can come to little less than two Millions of Money.

There are yet behind many Particulars of a distinct Nature from those that have been spoken of; some whereof are very wonderful, and call for a very serious Observation of them.

In the Cities of *London* and *Westminster*, especially on the Bridge and near *Walingford-house*, several Persons were blown down one on the Top of another.

In *Hertfordshire*, a Man was taken up, carried a Pole in Length, and blown over a very high Hedge; and the like in other Places.

The Water in the River of *Thames*, and other Places, was in a very strange manner blown up into the Air: Yea, in the new Pond in *James's Park*, the Fish, to the Number of at least two Hundred, where blown out and lay by the Bank-side, whereof many were Eye-witnesses.

At *Moreclack* in *Surry*, the Birds, as they attempted to fly, were beaten down to the Ground by the Violence of the Wind.

At *Epping* in the County of *Essex*, a very great Oak was blown down, which of it felt was raised again, and doth grow firmly at this Day.

At *Taunton*, a great Tree was blown down, the upper Pare whereof rested upon a Brick or Stone-wall, and after a little time, by the Force of the Wind, the lower part of the Tree was blown quite over the Wall.

In the City of *Hereford*, several Persons were, by the Violence of the Wind, born up from the Ground; one Man (as it is credibly reported) at least six Yards.

The great Fane at *Whitehall* was blown down, and one of the four which were upon the *white Tower*, and two more of them strangely bent; which are to be seen at this Day, to the Admiration of all that behold them.

The several *Triamphant Arches* in the City of *London* were much shattered and torn; That in Leaden-ball-street lost the King's Arms, and many other rare Pieces that were affixed to it; That in *Cheapside*, which represented the Church, suffered very much by the Fury of the Storm; and a great Part of that in *Fleet street* (which represented Plenty) was blown down: but, blessed be God, none as we hear of were either killed or hurt by the Fall of it.

The Wind was so strong, that it blew down several Carts loaded with Hay in the Road between *Barnet* and *London*; and in other Roads leading to the City of *London*.

Norwich Coach, with four or six Horses, was not able to come towards *London*, but stayed by the way till the Storm was somewhat abated.

It is also credibly reported, 'That all, or some of the Heads which were set up upon *Westminster-Hall*, were that Day blown down.

There was a very dreadful Lightning which did at first accompany the Storm, and by it some of his Majesty's Household conceive that the Fire which happened at *Whitehall* that Morning, was kindled; as also that at *Greenwich*, by which (as we are informed) seven or eight Houses were burnt down.

Thus far the Author of Mirabilis Annis

'Tis very observable, that this Storm blew from the same Quarter as the last, and that they had less of it Northward than here; in which they were much alike.

Now as these Storms were perhaps very furious in some Places, yet they neither came up to the Violence of this, nor any way to be compar'd for the

Extent, and when ruinous in one Country, were hardly heard of in the next.

But this terrible Night shook all Europe; and. how much farther it extended, he only knows who *has his way in the Whirlwind, and in the Storm, and the Clouds are the Dust of his Feet*.

As this Storm was first felt from the West, some have conjectured that the first Generation or rather Collection of Materials, was from the Continent of *America*, possibly from that part of *Florida* and *Virginia* where, if we respect natural Causes, the Confluence of Vapours rais'd by the Sun from the vast and unknown Lakes and Inland Seas of Water, which as some relate are incredibly large as well as nurmerous, might afford sufficient Matter for the Exhalation; and where time adding to the Preparation, God, who has generally confin'd his Providence to the Chain of natural Causes, might muster together those Troops of Combustion till they made a sufficient Army duly proportion'd to the Expedition design'd.

I am the rather inclin'd to this Opinion, because we are told, they felt upon that Coast an unusual Tempest a few Days before the fatal 27th of *November*.

I confess, I have never fludied the Motion of the Clouds so nicely, as to calculate how long time this Army of Terror might take up in its furious March; possibly the Velocity of its Motion might not be so great at its first setting out as it was afterward, as a Horse that is ro run a Race does not immediately put himself into the height of his Speed: and tho' it may be true, that by the length of the way the force of the Wind spends it self, and so by degrees ceases as the Vapour finds more room for Dilation; besides, yet we may suppose a Conjunction of some confederate Matter which might fall in with it by the way, or which meeting it at its Arrival here, might join Forces in executing the Commission receiv'd from above, all natural Causes being allow'd a Subserviency to the Direction of the great supream Cause; yet where the vat Collection of Matter had its first Motion, as it did not all take Motion in one and the same moment, so when all the Parts had felt the Influence, as they advanc'd and press'd those before them, the Violence must increase in proportion: and thus we may conceive that the Motion might not have arriv'd at its Meridian Violence till it reach'd our Hand; and even then it blew some Days with more than common fury, yet much less than that last Night of its force; and even that Night the Violence was not at its extremity till about an hour before Sun-rise, and then it continued declining, tho' it blew a full Storm for four Days after it.

Thus Providence, by whose special Direction the Quantity and Conduct of this Judgement was manag'd, seem'd to proportion things so, as that by the course of things the proportion of Matter being suited to Diltance of Place, the Motion shou'd arrive at its full Force just at che Place where its Execution was to begin.

As then our Island was the first, this way, to receive the Impressions of the violent Motion, it had the terriblest Effects here; and continuing its steady Course, we find it 'carried a true Line clear over the Continent of *Europe*, travers'd *England*, *France*, *Germany*, the *Baltick* Sea, and passing the Norther Continent of *Sweedland*, *Finland*, *Muscovy*, and part of *Tartary*, must at last lose it self in the vast. Northern Ocean, where Man never came, and Ship never sail'd; and its Violence cou'd have no effect, but upon the vast Mountains of Ice and the huge Drifts of Snow, in which Abyss of Moisture and Cold it is very probable the Force of it was check'd, and the World restor'd to Calmness and Quiet: and in this Circle of Fury it might find its End not far off from where it had its Beginning, the Fierceness of the Motion perhaps not arriving to a Period, till having pass'd the Pole, it reached again the Northern Parts of *America*.

The Effects of this impetuous Course, are the proper Subjects of this Book; and what they might be before our Island felt its Fury, who can tell? Those unhappy Wretches who had the misfortune to meet it in its first Approach, can tell us little, having been hurried by its irresistible Force directly into Eternity: how many they are, we cannot pretend to give an Account; we are told of about seventeen Ships, which having been out at Sea are never heard of: which is the common way of Discourse of Ships founder'd in the Ocean: and indeed all we can say of them is, the fearful Exit they have made among the Mountains of Waters, can only be duly reflected on by those who have seen those Wonders of God in the Deep.

Yet I cannot omit here to observe, That this Loss was in ail probability much less than it would otherwise have been; because the Winds having blown with very great Fury, at the same Point, for near fourteen Days before the Violence grew to its more uncommon height, all those Ships which were newly gone to Sea were force'd back, of which some were driven into *Plymouth* and *Falmouth* who had been above a hundred and fifty Leagues at Sea; others, which had been farther, took Sanctuary in *Ireland*.

On the other hand, All those Ships which were homeward bound, and were within 500 Leagues of the *English* Shore, had been hurried so furiously on *afore it (a the Seamen say)* that they had reach'd their Port before the Extremity of the Storm came on; so that the Sea was as it were swept clean of all Shipping, those which were coming home were blown home before their time; those that had attempted to put to Sea, were driven back again insight of all their Skill and Courage: for the Wind had blown so very hard, directly into the Channel, that there was no possibility of their keeping the Sea whose Course was not right afore the Wind.

On the other hand, these two Circumstances had fill'd all our Ports with unusual Fleets of Ships, either just come home or outward-bound, and consequently the Loss among them was very terrible; and the Havock it made among them, tho' it was not so much as every body, expected, was such as no Age or Circumstance can ever parallel, and we hope will never feel again.

Nay, so high the Winds blew even before *that we call the Storm*, that had not that intolerable Tempest follow'd so soon after, we should have counted those Winds extraordinary high: and any one may judge of the Truth of this from these few Particulars; That the Russia Fleet, compos'd of near a hundred Sail, which happen'd to be then upon the Coast, was absolutely dispers'd and scatter'd, some got into Newcastle, some into Hull, and some into Yarmouth Roads; two founder'd in the Sea; one or two more run ashore, and were lost; and the Reserve Frigat, their Convoy, founder'd in *Yarmouth* Roads, all her Men being loft, and no Boat from the Shore durst go off to relieve her, tho' it was in the Day-time, but all her Men perished.

In the same previous Storms the Man of War was lost off of *Harwich*; but by the help of smaller Vessels most of her Men were sav'd.

And so high the Winds blew for near a Fortnight, that no Ship stirr'd out of Harbour; and all the Vessels, great or small, that were out at Sea, made for some Port or other for shelter.

In this juncture of time it happen'd, that together with the *Russia* Fleet, a great Fleet of Laden Colliers, near 400 Sail, were just put out of the River Tine: and these being generally deep and unweildy Ships, met with hard measure; tho' not so fatal to them as was expected: such of them as could run in for *Humber*, where a great many were lost afterwards, as I shall relate in its course; some got shelter under the high Lands of *Cromer* and the Northern Shores of the County of *Norfolk*, and the greater number reach'd into *Yarmouth* Roads.

So that when the Great Storm came, our Ports round the Sea-Coast of *England* were exceeding full of Ships of all sorts: a brief account whereof take as follows.

At *Grinsby Hull*, and the other Roads of the *Humber*, lay about 80 Sail, great and small, of which about 50 were Colliers, and part of the *Russia* Fleet as aforesaid.

In *Yarmouth* Roads there rode at least 400 Sail, being most of them Laden Colliers, *Russia* Men, and Coasiters from *Lynn* and *Hull*.

In the River of Thames, at the Wore, lay about 12 Sail of the Queen's hir'd Ships and Store-ships, and only two Men of War.

Sir *Cloudsly Shovel* was just arriv'd from the *Mediterranean* with the Royal Navy: Part of them lays at St. *Hellens*, part in the *Downs*, and with 12 of the biggest Ships he was coming round the Foreland to bring them into *Chatham*; and when the Great Storm tates was at an Anchor at the Gunfleet, from whence the *Association* was driven off from Sea as fer as the Coast of *Norway*: What became of the rest, I refer to a Chapter by it self.

At *Gravesend* there rode five *East India* Men, and about 30 Sail of so ther Merchant-men, all outward bound.

In the *Downs* 160 Sail of Merchant Ships outward bound, besides that part of the Fleet which came in with Sir *Cloudsly Shovel*, which consisted of about 18 Men of War, wath Tenders and Victuallers.

At *Portsmouth* and *Cowes* there lay three Fleets; first, a Fleet of Transports and Tenders, who with Admiral *Dilks* brought the Forces from *Ireland* that were to accompany the King of *Spain* to *Lisbon*, secondly, a great Fleet of Victuallers, Tenders, Store-ships, and Transports, which lay ready for the same Voyage, together with about 40 Merchant-ships, who lay for the benefit of their Convoy; and the third Article was, the Remainder of the Grand Fleet which came in with Sir *Cloudsly Shovel*; in all almost 300 Sail, great and small.

In *Plymouth* Sound, *Falmouth* and *Milford* Havens, were particularly several small Fleets of Merchant-ships, driven in for Shelter and Harbour from the Storm, most homeward bound from the Islands and Colonies of *America*.

The *Virginia* Fleet, *Barbadoes* Fleet, and some *East India* Men, lay scatter'd in all our Ports, and in *Kinsale* in *Ireland* there lay near 80 Sail, homeward bound and richly laden.

At Bristol about 20 Sail of home-bound *West India* Men, not yet unladen.

In *Holland*, the Fleet of Transports for *Lisbon* waited for the King of *Spain*, and several *English* Men ot War lay at *Helvoet Sluice*; the *Dutch* Fleet from the *Texel* lay off of *Cadsandt*, with their Forces on Board, under the Admiral *Callenverge*. Both these Fleets made 180 Sail.

I think I may very safely affirm, That hardly in the Memory of the oldeft Man living, was a juncture of Time when an Accident of this nature could have happen'd, that so much Shipping, laden out and home, ever was in Port one time.

No Man will wonder that the Damages to this Nation were so Great, if they consider these unhappy Circumfances: it sho'd, wonder be at, that we have no more Disasters to account to Posterity, but that the Navigation of this Country came off so well.

And therefore some People have excus'd the Extravagancies of the *Paris Gazetter*, who orb firm'd in Print, that there Was 30000 Sea-men lost in the several Ports of *England*, see 300 Sail of Ships; which they say was a probal Conjecture: and that considering the multitude of Shipping, the Openness of the Roads in the *Downs*, *Yarmouth*, and the *Nore*, and the prodigious Fury of the Wind, any Man would have guess'd the same as he.

'Tis certain, It is a thing wonderful to consider, that especially in the *Downs* and *Yarmouth* Roads any thing shou'd be safe: all Men that know how wild a Road the first is, and what Crowds of Ships there lay in the last; how almost every thing quitted the Road; and nets Anchor nor Cable would hold; must wonder what Shift or what Course the Mariners could direct themselves to for Satety.

Some which had not a Mast standing, nor an Anchor or Cable left them, went out to Sea wherever the Winds drove them: and lying like a Trough in the Water, wallow'd about till the Winds abated; and after were driven some into one Port, some into another, as Providence guided them.

In short, Horror and Confusion seiz'd upon all, whether on Shore or at Sea: No Pen can describe it, no Tongue can express it, no Thought conceive it, unless some of those who were in the Extremity of it; and who, being touch'd with a due sense of the sparing Mercy of their Maker, retain the deep Impressions of his Goodness upon their Minds, tho' the Danger be past: and of those I doubt the Number is but few.

OF THE
EFFECTS
OF THE
STORM

The particular dreadful Effects of this Tempest, are the Subject of the ensuing Part of this History: And tho' the Reader is not to expect that all the Particulars can be put into this Account, and perhaps many very remarkable Passages may never come to our Knowledge, yet as we have endeavour'd to furnish our selves with the most authentick Accounts we could from all Parts of the Nation, and a great many worthy Gentlemen have contributed their Assistance in various, and some very exact Relations and curious Remarks; so we pretend, not to be meanly furnish'd for this Work.

Some Gentlemen, whose Accounts are but of common and trivial Damages, we hope will not take it ill from the Author, if they are not inserted at large; for that we are willing to put anything here common with other Accidents of nature; or which may not be worthy of a History and a Historian to record them; nothing but what may serve to assist in convincing Posterity that this was the most violent Tempest the World ever saw.

From hence 'twill toll that those Towns who only had their Houses until'd, their Barns and Hovels levell'd with the Ground, and the like, will find very little notice taken of them in this Account; because if these were to be the Subject of story, I presume it must be equally voluminous with *Fox*,[1] *Grimston*,[2] *Holinshead*[3] or *Stow*.[4]

Nor shall I often trouble the Reader with the Multitude or Magnitude of Trees blown down, whole Parks ruin'd, fine Walks defac'd, and Orchards laid flat, and the like: and tho' I had, myself, the Curios-

1   John Foxe (1516/17 - 1587), an English historian and martyrologist, best known for Foxe's Book of Martyrs, a history of Christian martyrdom, particularly focusing on Protestant persecution. —Ed.

2   Sir Edward Grimston (1600 - 1640s), an English politician and translator known for his historical writings.—Ed.

3   Raphael Holinshed (d. 1580 or 1582), an English chronicler best known for Holinshed's Chronicles, a massive historical compilation that served as a key source for William Shakespeare's history plays. —Ed.

4   John Stow (1524/25–1605), an English historian and antiquarian, famous for his Survey of London, which provides an invaluable record of Elizabethan London. —Ed.

ity to count the Number of Trees, in a Circuit I rode, over most part of *Kent*, in which being tired with the Number, I left off reckoning after I had gone on to 17000; and tho' I have great reason to believe I did not observe one half of the Quantity; yet in some Parts of *England*, as in *Devonshire* especially, and the Counties of *Worcester*, *Gloucester*, and *Hereford*, which are full of very large Orchards of Fruit-Trees, they had much more mischief:

In the Pursuit of this Work, I shall divide it into the following Chapters or Sections, that I May put it into as good Order as possible.

1. Of the Damage in the City of London, &c.
2.   in the Countries.
3.⎫ *On the water* ⎧ in the Royal Navy.
4.⎭   ⎩ to Shipping in general.
5:                             by Earthquake,
6.   by High Tides.
7. Remarkable Providences and Deliverances.
8. Hardned and blasphemous Contemners both of the-Storm and its Effects.
9. Some Calculations of Damage sustain'd.
10. The Conclusion.

We had design'd a Chapter for the Damages abroad, and have been at no small Charge to procure the Particulars from foreign Parts, which are now doing in a very authentick manner: but as the World has been long expecting this Work, and several Gentlemen who were not a little contributing to the Information of the Author, being unwilling to stay any longer for the Account, it was resolved to put it into the Press without any farther Delay: and if the foreign Accounts can be obtain'd in time, they shall be a Supplement to the Work; if not, some other Method shall be found out to make them publick.

I

Of the Damage in the City
of London and Parts Adjacent

Indeed the City was a strange Spectacle, the Morning after the Storm, as soon as the People could put their Heads out of Doors: though I believe, every Body expected the Destruction was bad enough; yet I questiom very much, if any Body believed the Hundredth Part of what they saw.

The Streets lay so covered with Tiles and Slates, from the Tops of the Houses, especially in the Out-parts, chat the Quantity is incredible: and the Houses were so universally stript, that all the Tiles in Fifty Miles round would be able to repair but a small Part of it.

Something may be guest at on this Head, from the sudden Rise of the Price of Tiles; which rise from 21 *s*. per Thousand to 64. for plain Tiles; and from 50 *s*. per Thousand for Pantiles, to 10 *l*. and Bricklayers Labour to 5 *s*. per Day: And tho' after the first Hurry the Prices fell again, it was not that the Quantity was supply'd; but because,

1st. The Charge was so extravagant, that an universal Neglect of themselves, appear'd both in Landlord and Tenant; an incredible Number of Houses remain'd all the Winter uncovered, and expos'd to all the Inconveniences of Wet and Cold; and are so even at the Writing of this Chapter.

2. Those People who found it absolutely necessary to cover their Houses, but were unwillling to go to the extravagant Price of Tiles; chang'd their Covering to that of Wood, as a present Expedient, till the Season for making of Tiles should come on; and the first Hurry being over, the Prices abate: and 'tis on this Score, that we see, to this Day, whole Ranks of Buildings, as in *Christ-Church Hospital*, the *Temple*, *Asks-Hospital*, *Old-street*, Hogsaen-Squares, and infinite other Places, covered entirely with Deal Boards; and are like to continue so, perhaps a Year or two longer, for Want of Tiles.

These two Reasons reduc'd the Tile-Merchants to fell at a more moderate Price: But 'tis not an irrational Suggestion, that all the Tiles which shall be made this whole Summer, will not repair the Damage in the covering of Houses within the Circumference of the City, and Ten Miles round.

The next Article in our Street Damiage was, the Fall of Chimneys; and as the Chinineys in the City Buildings are built in large Stacks, the Houses being so high, the Fall of them had the more Power, by their own Weight, to demolish the Houses they fell upon.

'Tis not possible to give a distinct Account of the Number, or particular Stacks of Chimneys, which fell to this fatal Night; but the Reader may guess by this Particular, that in *Cambray-House*, commonly so called, a great House near *Islington*, belonging to the Family of the Conptons, Earls of Northampton, but now let out into Tenements; the Collector of these Remarks counted Eleven or Thirteen Stacks of Chimneys, either wholly thrown in, or the greatrest Parts of them at least, what was expos'd to the Wind, blown off, I have heard Persons, who pretended to observe the Desolation of that terrible Night very nicely; and who, by what they had seen and enquired into, thought themselves capable of making some Calculations, affirm, They could give an Account of above Two Thousand Stacks of Chimneys blown down in and about *London*; besides Gable Ends of Houses, some whole Roofs, and Sixteen or Twenty whole Houses in the Out-Parts.

Under the Disaster of this Article, it seems most proper to place the Loss of the Peoples Lives, who fell in this Calamity; since most of those, who had the Misfortune to be killed, were buried, or beaten to Pieces with the Rubbish of the several Stacks of Chimneys that fell.

Of these, our Weekly Bills of Mortality gave us an Account of Twenty One; besides such as were drown'd in the River, and never found: and besides above Two Hundred People very much wounded and maim'd.

One Woman was kill'd by the Fall of a Chimney in or near the Palace of St. *James*'s, and a Stack of Chimneys falling in the new unfinish'd Building there, and carried away a Piece of the Coin of the House.

Nine Souldiers were hurt, with the Fall of the Roof of the Guard-house at *Whitehall*, but mone of them died.

A Distiller in *Duke-street*, with his Wife, and Maid-servant, were all buried in the Rubbish of a Stack of Chimneys, which forced all the Floors, and broke down to the Bottom of the House; the Wife was taken out alive, though very much bruised, but her Husband and the Maid lost their Lives.

One Mr. *Dyer*, a Plaisterer in Fetter-Lane, finding the Danger he was in by the shaking of the House, jumpe out of Bed to save himself; and had, in all Probability, Time enough to have got out of the House, but staying to strike a Light, a Stack of Chimneys fell in upon him, kill'd him, and wounded his Wife.

Two Boys at one Mr. *Purefoy*'s, in *Cross-street Hatton-Garden*, were both kill'd, and buried in the Rubbith of a Stack of Chimneys; and a third very much wounded.

A Woman in *Jewin-street*, and Two Persons more near *Aldersgate-street*, were kill'd; the first, as it is reported, by venturing to run out of the House into the Street; and the other Two by the Fall of a House.

In *Threadneedle-street*, one Mr. *Simpson*, a scrive-ner being in Bed and fast asleep, heard nothing of the Storm; but the rest of the Family being more sensible of Danger, some of them went up, and wak'd him; and telling him their own Apprehentions, press'd him to rise; but he too fatally sleepy, and consequently unconcern'd at e Danger, told them, he did not apprehend any Thing; and so, notwithstanding all their Persuasions, could nor be prevailed with to rise; they had not been gone many Minutes out of his Chamber, before the Chimneys fell in, broke through the Roof over him, and kill'd him in his Bed.

A Carpenter in *White-Cross-street* was kill'd almost in the same Manner, by a Stack of Chimneys of the *Swan* Tavern, which fell into his House: it was reported, That his Wife earnestly desir'd him not to go to Bed; and had prevail'd upon him to sit up till near two a Clock, but then finding himself very heavy, he would go to Bed against all his Wife's Intreaties; after which, she wak'd him, and desir'd him to rise, which he refus'd, being something angry for being disturb'd; and going to sleep again, was Kill'd in his Bed: and his Wife, who would lot go to Bed, escap'd.

In this Manner, our Weekly Bills gave us an Account of Twenty One Persons kill'd in the City of London, and Parts adjacent.

Some of our printed Accounts give us larger arid plainer Accounts of the Loss of Lives, than I will venture to affirm for Truth; as of several Houses near *Moor-Fields* levell'd with the Ground: Fourteen People drowned in a Wherry going to Gravesend, and Five in a Wherry from *Chelsey*. Not that it is not very probable to be true; but as I resolve not to hand any thing to Posterity, but what comes very well attested, I omit such Relations as I have not extraordinary Assurance as to the Fact.

The Fall of Brick-Walls, by the Fury of this Tempest, in and about *London*, would make a little Book of it self; and as this affects the Out-Parts chiefly, where the Gardens and Yards are wall'd in, so few such have escap'd: at St. *James*'s a considerable part of the Garden Wall; at *Greenwich Park* there are several pieces of the Wall down for an Hundred Rods in a Place; and some much more, at. *Battersey*, *Chelsey*, *Putney*, at *Clapham*, at *Deptford*, at *Hackney*, *Islington*, *Hogsden*, *Woods Close* by St. *John's Street*, and on every side the City, the Walls of the Gardens have generally felt the Shock, and lie flat on the Ground twenty, thirty Rod of walling in a Place.

The publick Edifices of the City come next under our Consideration; and these have had their Share in the Fury of this terrible Night.

A part of her Majesty's Palace, as is before observ'd, with a Stack of Chimneys in the Centre of the new Buildings, then not quite finished, fell with such a terrible Noise as very much alarm'd the whole Houshold.

The Roof of the Guard-house at *Whitehall*, as is also observ'd before, was quite blown off; and the great Vane, or Weather-Cock at *Whitehall* blown down.

The Lead, on the Tops of the Churches and other Buildings, was in many Places roll'd up like a Roll of Parchment, and blown in some Places clear off from the Buildings; as at *Westminster Abby*, St. *Andrews Holbourn*, *Christ-Church Hospital*, and abundance of other Places.

Two of the new built Turrets, on the Top of St. *Mary Aldermary Church*, were blown off, whereof One fell upon the Roof of the Church: of Eight Pinnacles on the Top of St. *Albans Woodstreet*, Five of them were blown down: Part of One of the Spires of St. *Mary Overies* blown off; Four Pinnacles on the Steeple of St. *Michael Crooked Lane* blown quite off: The Vanes and Spindles of the Weather-Cocks, in many Places, bent quite down; as on St. *Michael Cornhil*, St. *Sepulchres*, the *Tower*, and divers other Places.

It was very remarkable, that the Bridge over the *Thames* received but little Damage, and not in Proportion to what in common Reason might be expected; since the Buildings there and high, and are not sheltered, as they are in the Streets, one by another.

If I may be allow'd to give this Philosophical Account of it, I hope it may not be absurd; that the Indraft of the Arches underneath the Houses giving Vent to the Air, it past there with a more

than common Current; and consequently relieved the Buildings, by diverting the Force of the
Storm: I ask Pardon of the ingenious Reader for
this Opinion, if it be not regular, and only present it to the World for Want of a better; if those
better furnished *that Way* will supply us with a
truer Account, I shall withdraw mine, and submit to theirs. The Fact however is certain, that the
Houses on the Bridge did not suffer in Proportion
to the other Places: though all must allow, they do
not seem to be stronger built, than other Streets of
the same sort.

Another Observation. I cannot but make; to
which, as I have Hundreds of Instances, so I have
many more Witnesses to the Truth of Fact, and
the uncommon Experiment has made it the more
observ'd,

The Wind blew, during the whole Storm, between the Points of S. W. and N. W. not that I mean
it blew at all these Points, but I take a Latitude of
Hight Points to avoid Exceptions, and to confirm
my Argument; since what I am insisting upon,
could not be a natural Cause from the Winds blowing in any of those particular Points.

If a Building stood North and South, it must
be a Consequence that the East-side Slope of the
Roof must be the Lee-side, lie out of the Wind, be
weather'd by the Ridge, and consequently receive
no Damage in a direct Line.

But against this rational way of arguing, we are
convinced by Demonstration and Experiment, af-

ter which Argument must be silent. It was not in one Place or Two, but in many Places; that where a Building stood ranging North and South, the Sides or Slopes of the Roof to the East and the West, the East-side of the Roof would be stript and untiled by the Violence of the Wind; and the West Side, which lay open to the Wind, be found and un-couch'd.

This, I conceive, mut happen either where the Building had some open Part, as Windows or Doors to receive the Wind in the Inside, which be-ing pusht forward by the succeeding Particles of the Air, must force its Way forward, and so lift off the Tiling on the Leward Side of the Building; or it must happen from the Position of such Building near some other higher Place or Building, where the Wind being repuls'd, must be forc'd back again in Eddies; and consequentiy taking the Tiles from the lower Side of the Roof, rip them up with the more Ease.

However it was, it appear'd in many Places, the Windward Side of the Roof would be whole, and the Leeward Side, or the Side from the Wind, be untiled; in other Places, a high Building next the Wind has been not much hurt, and a lower Build-ing on the Leeward Side of the high One clean ript, and hardly a Tile left upon it: this is plain in the Building of Christ Church Hospital in London, where the Building on the Wet and South Side of the Cloyster was at least Twenty Five Foot higher than the East Side, and yet the Roof of the lower

Side on the East was quite untiled by the Storm, and remains at the Writing of This covered with Deal Boards above an Handred Foor in Length.

The blowing down of Trees may come in for another Article in this Part; of which, in Proportion to the Quantity, here was as much as in any Pare of *England*: Some printed Accounts tell us of Seventy Trees in *Moorfields* blown down, which may be true; but that some of them were Three Yards about, as is affirmed by the Authors, I cannot allow: above a Hundred Elms in St. *James's Park*, some whereof were of such Growth, as they tell us they were planted by Cardinal *Woolsey*; whether that Part of it be true ot not, is little to the Matter, but only to imply that they were very great Trees: about *Baums*, commonly call'd *Whitmore house*, there were above Two Hundred Trees blown down, and some of them of extraordinary Size broken off in the middle.

And 'twas observ'd, that in the Morning after the Storm was abated, it blew so hard, the Women, who usually go for Milk to the Cow-keepers in the Villages round the City, were not, able to go along with their Pails on their Heads; and One, that was more hardy than the rest, was blown away by the Fury of the Storm, and forced into a Pond, but by strugling hard got out, and avoided being drowned; and some that ventured out with Milk the Evening after, had their Pails and Milk blown off from their Heads.

'Tis impossible to enumerate the Particulars of the Damage suffered, and of the Accidents which happened under these several Heads, in and about the City of London: The Houses looked like Skeletons, and an universal Air of Horror seem'd to fit on the Countenances of the People; all Business seem'd to be laid aside for the Time, and People were generally intent upon getting Help to repair their Habitations.

It pleased God so to direct things, that there fell no Rain in any considerable Quantity, except what fell the same Night or the ensuing Day, for near Three Weeks after the Storm, though it was a Time of the Year that is generally dripping. Had a wet Rainy Season followed the Storm, the Damage which would have been suffered in and about this City to Houshold Goods, Furniture and Merchandise, would have been incredible, and might have equall'd all the the rest of the Calamity: but the Weather prov'd fair and temperate for near a Month after the Storm, which gave People a great deal of: Leisure in providing themselves Shelter, and for tilying their Houses against the Accidents of Weather by Deal Boards, old Tiles, Pieces of Sail Cloth, Tarpaulin, and the like.

II

Of the Damage in the Country

s the Author of this was an Eye-witness and Sharer of the Particulars in
the former Chapter so, to furnish the
Reader with Accounts as authentick,
and which he has as much cause to
depend upon as if he had seen them, he has the
several Particulars following from like Eye-witnesses, and that in such a manner, as I think their
Testimony is not to be question'd, most of the Gentlemen being of Piety and Reputation.

And as a Publication was made to desire all
Persons who were willing to contribute to the forwarding this Work, and to transmit the Memory of

so signal a Judgmentt to Posterity, that they would be pleas'd to send up such authentick Accounts of the Misichiefs, Damages, and Disasters in their respective Countries that the World might rely on; it cannot, without a great breach of Charity, be suppos'd that Men mov'd by such Principles, without any private of Advantage, would forge any a pose upon the World, and abuse Ages to come.

Interest, Parties, Strife, Faction, and particular Malice, with all the scurvy Circumstances attending such things; may prompt Men to strain a Tale beyond its real Extent; but, that Men shou'd invent a Story to amuse Posterity, in a case where they have no manner of Motive, where the only Design is to preserve the Remembrance of Divine Vengeance, and put our Children in mind of God's Judgments upon their sinful Fathers, this would be telling a Lye for God's sake, and doing Evil for the sake of it self, which is a step beyond the Devil.

Besides, as most of our Relators have not only given us their Names, and sign'd the Accounts they have sent, but have also given us Leave to hand their Names down to Posterity with the Record of the Relation they give, we would hope no Man will be so uncharitable to believe that Men would be forward to set their Names to a voluntary Untruth, and have themselves recorded to Posterity to having, without Motion, Hope, Reward, or any other reason, impos'd a Falsity upon the World, and dishonour'd our Relation with the useless Banter of an Untruth.

We cannot therefore but think, that as the Author believes himself sufficiently back'd by the Authority of the Vouchers he presents, so after what has been here premis'd, no Man will have any room to suspect us of Forgery.

The ensuing Relation therefore, as to Damages in the Country, shall consist chiefly of Letters from the respective Places where such things have happen'd; only that as all our Letters are not concise enough to be printed as they are, where it is otherwise the Letter is digested into a Relation only; in which the Reader is assur'd we have always kept close to the matter of fact.

And first, I shall present such Accounts as are entire, and related by Men of Letters: principally by the Clergy; which shall be given you in their own Words.

The first is from *Stowmarket* in *Suffolk*, where, by the Violence of the Storm, the finest Spire in that County, and but new built, viz. within thirty Years, was overthrown, and fell upon the Church. The Letter is sign'd by the reverend Minister of the Place, and vouched by two of the principal Inhabitants, as follows.

S I R,

Having seen an Advertisement of a Design to perpetuate the Remembrance of the late dreadful Storm, by publishing a Collection of all the remarkable Accidents occasion'd by it, and supposing the Damage done to our Church to be none of the least, we were willing to contribute something to your Design, by sending you an Account thereof as follows.

We had formerly a Spire of Timber covered with Lead, of the height of 77 Foot; which being in danger of falling, was taken down: and in the Year 1674, with the Addition of 10 Loads of new Timber, 21 thousand and 8 hundred weight of Lead, a new one was erected, 100 Foot high from the Steeple, with a Gallery at the height of 40 Foot all open, wherein hung a Clock-Bell of between 2 and 3 hundred Weight. The Spire stood but 8 Yards above the Roof of the Church; and yet by the extreme Violence of the Storm, a little before 6 in the Morning the Spire was thrown down; and carrying with it all the Battlements on the East side, it fell upon the Church at the diffance of 28 Foot; for so much is the distance between the Steeple and the bell Breach, which is on the North-side of the middle Roof, of the length of 17, Foot, where it brake down 9 Spars clean, each 23 Foot long, and severally supported with very strong Braces. The Spire inclining to the North, fell cross the middle Wall, and broke off at the Gallery, the lower part falling in at the aforesaid Breach, and the upper upon the North isle, which is 24 Foot wide, with a flat Roof lately built, all new and very strong: It carried all before it from side to side, making a Breach 37 Foot long, breaking in sunder two large, Beams that went across, which were 12 Inches broad and 15 deep, besides several other smaller. Besides these two Breaches, there is a great deal of Damage done by the Fall of great Stones upon other parts of the Roof, as well as by the Wind's riving up the Lead, and a third part of the Pews broken all in pieces, every thing falling into the Church, except the Weather-cock, which was found in the Church-yard, at a considerable distance, in the great Path that goes cross by the East End of the Church. It will cost above 400 *l.* to make all good as it was before. There were 3 single Chimneys blown down, and a Stack of 4 more together, all about the same time; and some others so shaken, that they were forced to be pull'd down; but, we thank God, no boay hurt, tho' one Bed was broken in pieces that was very oft lain in: no body lay in it that Night. Most Houses suffered somerhing in their Tiling, and generally all round the Country, there is incredible Damage done to Churches, Houses, and Barns.

Samuel Farr, Vicar.
John Gaudy.
William Garrard.

From *Oxfordshire* we have an Account very authentick, and yet unaccountably strange: but the reverend Author of the Story being a Gentleman whose credit we Cannot dispute, in acknowledgment to his Civility, and for the Advantage of our true Delign, we give his Letter also *verbatim.*

S I R,

eeting with an Advertisement of yours in the *Gazette of Monday* last, I very much approved of the Design, thinking it might be a great Motive towards making People, when they hear the Fate of others, return Thanks to Almighty God for his Providence in preserving them. I accordingly was resolved to send you all I knew. The Place where I have for some time lived is *Besselsleigh*, in *Barkshire*, about four Miles S. W. of *Oxon*. The Wind began with us much about. One of the Clock in the Morning, and did not do much harm, only in untiling Houses, blowing down: a Chimney or two, without any Person hurt, and a few Trees: but what was the only thing that was strange, and to be observed, was a very tall Elm, which was found the next Morning standing, but perfectly twisted round; the Root a little loosen'd, but not torn up. But what happened the Afternoon preceding, is abundantly more surprizing, and is indeed the Intent of this Letter.

On *Friday* the 26th of *November*, in the Afternoon, about Four of the Clock, a Country Fellow came running to me in a great Fright, and very earnestly entreated me to go and see a Pillar, as he call'd it, in the Air, in a Field hard by. I went with the Fellow; and when I came, found it to be a Spout marching directly with the Wind: and I can think of nothing I can compare it to better than the Trunk of an Elephant, which it resembled, only much bigger, It was extended to a great Length, and swept the Ground as it went, leaving a Mark behind. It crossed a Field; and what was very strange (and which I should scarce have been induced to believe had I not my self seen it, besides several Country-men who were astonish'd at it) meeting with an Oak that stood towards the middle of the Field) snapped the Body of it asunder. Afterwards crossing a Road, it sucked up the Water that was in the Cart-ruts: then coming to an old Barn, it tumbled it down, and the Thatch that was on the Top was carried about by the Wind, which was then very high, in great confusion. After this I followed it no farther, and therefore saw no more of it. But a Parishioner of mine going from hence to *Hinkley*, in a Field about a quarter of a Mile off this Place, was on the sudden knock'd down, and lay upon the Place till some People came by and brought him home; and he is not yet quite recovered. Having examined him, by all I can collect both from the Time, and Place, and Manner of his being knock'd down, I must conclude it was done by the Spout, which, if its Force had not been much abated, had certainly kill'd him: and indeed I attribute his Illness more to the Fright, than the sudden Force with which he was struck down.

I will not now enter into a Dissartion on the Cause of Spouts, but by what I can understand they are caused by nothing but the Circumgyration of the Clouds, made by two contrary Winds meeting in a Point, and condensing the Cloud till it falls in the Shape we see it; which by the twisting Motion sucks up Water, and doth much Mischief to Ships at Sea, where they happen oftner than at Land. Whichever of the two Winds prevails, as in the above-mentioned was the S. W. at last dissolves and dissipates the Cloud, and then the Spout disappears.

This is all I have to communicate to you, wishing you all imaginable Success in your Collection. Whether you insert this Account, I leave wholly to your own Discretion; but can assure you, that to most of these things, tho' very surprizing, I was my self an Eye-witness. I am,

SIR,
Your humble Servant,
Joseph Ralton.

Dec. 12. 1703.

The judicious Reader will-observe here, that this strange Spout, or Cloud, or what else it may be call'd, was seen the Evening before the great Storm: from whence is confirm'd what I have said before of the violent Agitation of the Air for some time before the Tempest.

A short, but very regular Account, from *Northampton*, the Reader may take in the following Letter; the Person being of undoubted Credit and Reputation in the Town, and the Particulars very well worth remark,

S I R,

Having seen in the *Gazettee* an Intimation, there would be a Memorial drawn up of the late terrible Wind, and the Effects of it, and that the Composer desired Informations from credible Persons, the better to enable hint to do the same, I thought good to intimate what happen'd in this Town, and its. Neighbourhood: 1. The Weather-cock of *All-Saints* Church being placed on a mighty Spindle of Iron, was bowed together, and made useless. Many Sheets of Lead on that Church, as also on St. *Giles*'s and St. *Sepulchres*, rowled up like a Scroll. Three Windmills belonging to the Town blown down; to the Amazement of all Beholders; the mighty upright Pot below the Floor of the Mills being snapt in two like a Reed. Two entire Stacks of Chimneys in a House uninhabited fell on two several Roofs, and made a most amazing Ruin in the Chambers, Floors, and even to the lower Windows and Wainscot, splitting and tearing it as if a Blow by Gun-powder had happen'd. The Floods at this instant about the South Bridge, from a violent S.W. Wind, rose to a great and amazing height; the Wind coming over or a-thwart large open Meadows, did exceeding damage in that part of the Town, by blowing down some whole Houses, carrying whole Roofs at once into the Streets, and very many lesser Buildings of Tanners, Fell-mongers, Dyers, Glue-makers, &c. yet, through the Goodness of God, no Person killed or maimed: the mighty Doors of the Sessions-houses barra'd and lock'd, forced open, whereby the Wind entring, made a miserable Havock of the large and lofty Windows: a Pinnacle on the *Guild-hall*, with the Fane, was also blown down. To speak of Houses shatter'd, Corn-ricks and Hovels blown from their Standings, would be endless. In Sir *Thomas Samwell*'s Park a very great-headed Elm was blown over the Park-Wall into the Road, and yet never touched the Wall, being carried some Yards. I have confined my self to this Town. If the Composer finds any thing agreeable to his Design, he may use it or dismiss it at his Discretion. Such Works of Providence are worth recording. I am

> *Your loving friend,*
> Ben. Bullivant.

Northampton,
Dec. 12. 1703.

The following Account from *Berkly* and other Places in *Gloucestershire* and *Somersetshire,* &c. are the sad Effects of the prodigious Tide in the *Severn.* The Wind blowing directly into the Mouth of that Channel we Call the *Severn* Sea; forced the Waters up in such quantity, that 'tis allow'd the Flood was eight Foot higher than ever was known in the Memory of Man; and at one Place, near *Huntspill*, it drove several Vessels a long way upon the Land; from whence, no succeeding Tide rising to near that height, they can never be gotten off: as will appear in the two following Letters.

S I R,

This Parish is a very large one in the County of *Gloucester*, on one Side whereof runneth the River *Severn*, which by Reason of the Violence of the late Storm beat down and tore to pieces the Sea Wall (which is made of great Stones, and Sticks which they call Rouses, a Yard and half long, about the Bigness of ones Thigh rammed into the Ground as firm as possible) in many Places, and levell'd it almost with the Ground, forcing vast Quantities of Earth a great Distance from the Shore, and Stones, many of which were above a Hundred Weight: and hereby the *Severn* was let in above a Mile over one part of the Parish, and did great Damage to the Land; it carried away one House which was by the Sea-side, and a Gentleman's Stable, wherein was a Horse, into the next Ground; and then the Stable fell to pieces, and so the Horse came out. There is one thing more remarkable in this Parish, and 'tis this: 'Twenty Six Sheets of Lead, hanging all together, were blown off from the middle Isle of our Church, and were carried over the North Isle, which is a very large one, without touching it; and into the Church-yard ten Yards distant from the Church; and they were took up all joyned together as they were on the Roof; the Plummer told me that the Sheets weighed each Three Hundred and a half one with another. This is what is most observable in our Parish; but I shall give you an Account of one thing (which perhaps you may have from other Hands) that happen'd, in another, call'd *Kingscote*, a little Village about Three Miles from *Tedbury*, and Seven from us; where *William Kingscote* Esq; has many Woods; among which was one Grove of very tall Trees, being each near Eighty Foot high; the which he greatly valued for the Tallness and Prospect of them, and therefore resolv'd never to cut them down: But it so happen'd, that Six Hundred of them, within the Compass of Five Acres were wholly blown down; (and suppos'd to be much at the same time) each Tree tearing up the Ground with its Root; so that the Roots of most of the Trees, with the Turf and Earth about them, stood up at least Fifteen or Sixteen Foot high; the lying down of which Trees is an amazing Sight to all Beholders. This Account was given by the Gentleman himself, whom I know very well, I have no more to add, but that I am, *Your humble Servant*, wishing you good Success in your Undertaking,

Henry Head, Vicar of *Berkly*.

Jan. 24

The Damage of the Sea-wall may amount to about five Hundred Pounds.

S I R,

Eceived a printed Paper sometime since, wherein I was desired to send you an Account of what happen'd in the late Storm: and I should have answered it sooner, but was willing to make some Enquiry first about this Country; it and by what I can hear or learn, the dismal Accident of our late Bishop and Lady was most remarkable; who Was killed by the Fall of two Chimney Stacks, which fell on the Roof, and drove it in upon my Lord's Bed, forced it quite through the next Flower down into the Hall, and buried them both in the Rubbish; and 'tis suppos'd my Lord was getting up, for he was found some Distance from my Lady, who was found in her Bed; but my Lord had his Morning Gown on, so that 'tis suppos'd he was coming from the Bed jut as it fell; We had likewise two small Houses blown flat down just as the People were gone out to a Neighbour's House; and several other Chimney Stacks fell down, and some through the Roof, but no other Accident as to Death in this Town or near it: abundance of Tiles are blown off, and likewise Thatch in and about this Town, and several Houses uncover'd, in the Country all about us, abundance of Apple and Elm Trees are rooted up by the Ground; and also abundance of Wheat and Hay-mows blown down: at *Huntspil*, about twelve Miles from this Town, there was Four or Five small Vessels drove a-shoar which remain there still, and 'tis suppos'd cannot be got of; and in the same Parish, the Tide broke in Breast high; but all the People escap'd only one Woman, who was drowned. These are all the remarkable Things that happen'd near us, as I can hear of; and is all, but my humble Service; and beg Leave to subscribe my self,

SIR,

Your most humble Serveant,
Edith Conyers.

Wells in Somersetshire,
Feb. 19. 1703.

S I R,

The Dreadful Storm did this Church but little Damage, but our Houses were terribly shaken hereabouts, and the Tide drowned the greatest part of the Sheep on our Common; as it likewise did, besides many Cows between this Place and *Bristol* 3; on the opposite Shore of *Glamorganshire,* as (I suppose -you may also know) it brake down part of Chepstow Bridge, o'er the *Wye,* In the midst of this Church-yard grew a vast Tree, thought to be the most large and flourishing Elm in the Land which was torn up by the Roots, some of which are really bigger than ones Middle, and several than a Man's Thigh; the Compass of them curiously interwoven with the

Earth, being from the Surface (or Turf) to the Basis, full an Ell[1] in Depth, and Eighteen Foot and half in the Diameter, and yet thrown up near Perpendicular; the Trunk, together with the loaden Roots, is well judg'd to be Thirteen Tun at least, and the Limbs to make Six Load of Billets with Faggots; and, about Two Years since, our Minister observ'd, that the circumambient Boughs dropt round above Two Hundred Yards: He hath given it for a Suncers Sear in our said Church, with this Inscription thereon; *Nov*. 27. A. D. 1703. *Miserere*, &c.

William Frith, Church Warden

Slimbridge near Severn
Dec. 28. 1703.

S I R,

y the late Dreadful Storm a considerable Breach was made in our Town Wall, and Part of the Church Steeple blown down; besides most of the Inhabitants suffered very much by untiling their Houses, &c. and abundance of Trees unrooted: at the same time our River overflowed, and drowned the low Grounds of both Sides the Town, whereby several Hundreds of Sheep were

---

1   An ell was an unit of measurement that in England was typically used in tailoring. It was 45 inches long or 1.143 metres. —Ed.

lost, and some Cattle; and one of our Market Boats lifted upon our Key. This is a true Account of most of our Damages. I am,

Your humble Servant,
William Jones.

Cardiff,
Jan. 10; 1703.

Honour'd Sir,

In Obedience to your Request I have here sent you a particular Account of the damages sustain'd in our Parish by the late Violent Storm: and because that of our Church is the most material which I have to impart to you, I shall therefore begin with it. It is the firmness of our Church which magnifies our present loss, for in the whole it is large and noble structure, compos'd within and without of Ashler curiously Wrought, and consisting of a stately Roof in the middle, and two Isles runing a considerable length from one end of it to the other, makes a very beautiful Figure. It is also adorn'd with 28 admired and Celebrated Widows, which for the variety and fineness of the Painted Glass that was in them, do justly attract the Eyes of all curious Travellers to inspect and behold them; nor is it more famous for its Glass than newly renown'd for the Beauty of its Seats and Paving, both being chiefly the noble ith of that pious and worthy Gentleman *Andrew Barker*, Esq; the late Deceas'd Lord of the Manor. So that all things consider'd, it does equal, at least, if not exceed, any Parochial Church in *England*. Now that part of it which most of all felt the fury of the Winds, was, a large middle West Window, in Dimension about 15 Foot wide, and 25 Food high: it represents the general Judgment, and is so fine a piece of Art, that 1500 *l.* has formerly been bidden for it, a price though very tempting, yet were the Parisishioners so just as honest as to refuse it. The upper part of this Window, just above the place where our Saviour's Picture is drawn sitting on a Rainbow, and the Earth his Foot-stool, is entirely ruin'd, and both sides are so shatter'd and torn, especially the left, that upon a general Computation, a fourth part, at least, is blown down and destroy'd. The like Fare has another West Window on the left side of the former, in Dimension about 10 Foot broad, and 15 Foot high, sustain'd; the upper half of which is totally broke, excepting one Stone Munnel. Now if this were but ordinary Glass, we might quickly compute what our repairs would Cost, but we the more lament our misfortune herein, because the Paint of these two, as of all the other Windows in out Church, is stain'd thro' the Body of the Glass; so that if that be true which is generaly said, that this Art is is lost, than have we an irretrievable loss. There are other damages about our Church, which, tho' not so great as the former, do yet as much testify how strong and boisterous the Winds were, for they unbedded Sheets of Lead upon the uppermost Rooff, and roll'd them up like so much paper. Over the Church-porch, a large Pinnacle and two Battlements were blown down upon the leads of it, but resting there, and their fall being short, these will be repair'd with little Cost. This is all I have to say concerning our Church: Our Houses come next to be considered, and here I may tell you, that (thanks be to God) the effects of the Storm were not so great as they have been in many other places; several Chimneys, and Tiles, and Slats, were thrown down, but no body kill'd or wounded. Some of the Poor, because their Houses were Thatch'd, were the greatest sufferers; but to be particular herein, would be very frivolous, as well as vexatious. One Instance of Note ought not to omitted; on *Saturday* the 26th, being the day after the Storm, about 2-a-Clock in the Afternoon, without any previous warning, a sudden flash of Lightning, with a short, with a violent clap of Thunder, immediately following it like the Discharge of Ordnance, fell upon a new and strong built House in the middle of our Town, and at the same time disjointed two Chimneys, melted some of the Lead of an upper Window, and struck the Mistress of the House into a Swoon, but this, as appear'd afterwards, prov'd the effect more of fear, than of any real considerable hurt to be found about her. I have nothing more to add, unless it be the fall of several Trees and Ricks of Hay amongst us, but these being so common every where, and not very many in number here, I shall Conclude this tedious Scrible, and Subscribe my self,

> SIR,
>
>> *Your most Obedient*
>> *and Humble Servant,*
>> Edw. Shipton, *Vic.*

Fairford, Gloucest.
January 170¼

The following Letters; tho in a homely stile, are written vs very honest plain and observing Persons, to whom entire Credit may be given.

BREWTON

S I R,

Some time since I received a Letter, from you, to give you an Account of the most particular Things that hapned in the late dreadful Tempest of Wind, and in the first Place is the Copy of a Letter from a Brother of mine, that was an Exciseman of *Axbridge*, in the West of our County of *Somerset*; these are his Words,

What I know of the Winds in these Parts, are, that it broke down many Trees, and that the

House of one *Richard Henden*, of *Charter-House* on *Mendip*, call'd *Piney*, was almost blown down, and in saving their House, they, and the Servants, and others, heard grievous Cries and Scrieches in the Air. The Tower of *Compton Bishop* was much shatter'd, and the Leads ney cover'd it were taken clean away, and laid flat in the Church-Yard: The House of John Cray of that place, received much and strange Damages, which together with his part in the Sea-wall, amounted to 500 *l*. Near the Salt-works in the Parish of *Burnham*, was driven five trading Vessels and Coiliers and Corn-dealers, betwixt *Wales* and *Bridgwater*, at least 100 Yards on Pasture Ground. In the North Marsh, on the sides of *Bristol* River, near *Ken* at *Walton Woodspring*, the Waters broke with such Violence, that it came six Miles into the Country drowning much Cattel, carrying away several Hay-ricks and Stacks of Corn: And at a Farm at *Churchill* near *Wrington*, it blew down 150 Elms that grew most in Rows, and were laid as Uniform as Soldiers lodge their Arms.

At *Cheddar* near *Axbridge*, was much harm done in Apple-trees, Houses, and such like; but what's worth remark, tho' not the very Night of the Tempest, a Company of wicked People being at a Wedding of one *Thomas Marshall, John*, the Father of the said *Thomas*, being as most of the Company was very Drunk, after much filthy Discourse while he was eating, a strange Cat pulling something from his Trenchard, he Cursing her, stoopt to take it and died immediately.

At *Brewton* what was most Remarkable, was this, chat one *John Dicer* of that Town, lay the Night as the Tempest was, in the Barn of one *John Seller*, the Violence of the Wind broke down the Roof of the Barn, but fortunately for him there was a Ladder which staid up a Raiter, which would have fell upon the said *John Dicer*: but he narrowly escaping being killed, did slide himself thro' the broken Roof, I and so got over the Wall without any great hurt. What hurt was done more about eal Town is not so consider able as in other Places; Such as blowing off the Thatch from a great many back Houses of the Town; for the Town is most tiled with a sort of heavy Tile, that the Wind had no power to move; there was some hurt done to the Church, which was not above 40 s. besides the Windows, where was a considerable damage, the Lady *Fitzharding*'s House standing by the Church, the Battlement with part of the Wall of the House was blows down, which 'tis said, above 20 Men with all their strength could not have thrown down; besides, a great many Trees in the Park on up by the Roots, and laid in very good Order one after another; it was taken notice a the Wind did not come in a full Body at once, but it came in several Gusts, as my self have taken Notice as I rid the Country, that in half a Miles rising I could not see a Tree down, nor much Hurt to Houses, then again I might for some space see the Trees down, and all the Houses shattred; and I have taken Notice that it run so all up the Country in such a Line as the Wind sat; about One of the Clock it turn'd to the North West, but at the beginning was at South West; I my self was up until One and then I went to Bed, but the highest of the Wind was after that, so that my Bed did shake with me.

What was about *Wincanton*, was, that one Mrs *Gapper* had 36 Elm-trees growing together in a Row, 35 of them was blown down; and one Edgehill of the same Town, and his Family being a Bed did arise, hearing the House begin to Crak, and got out of the Doors with his whole Family, and was soon as they were out of the Roof of the House fell in, and the Violence of the Wind took of the Children's Head-cloaths, that they never saw them afterwards.

At *Evercreech*, three Miles from *Brewton*, there were a poor Woman beg'd for Lodging ia the Barn of one *Edmond Peny* that same Night that the Storm was, she was wet the Day before in Travelling, so she hung up her Cloaths in the Barn, and lay in the Straw; but when the Storm came it blew down the Roof of the Barn where she lay, and she narrowly escaped with her Life, being much bruised, and got out almost naked through the Roof where it was broken most, and went to the dwelling House of the said Edmond Penny, and they did arise, and did help her to something to cover her, till they could get out her Cloaths; that place of *Evercreech* received a great deal of hurt in their Houses, which is too large to put here.

At *Batcomb* Easterly of *Everereech*, they had a great deal of Damage done as I said before, it lay exactly with the Wind from *Evercreech*, and both places received a the deal of Damage; there was one Widow *Walter* lived in a House by it self, the Wind carried away she Roof, and the Woman's pair of Bodice, that was never heard of again, and the whole Family escaped narrowly with their Lives; all, the Battlements of the Church on that side of the Tower next to the Wind was blown in, and a great deal of Damage done to the Church.

At *Shipton Mallet* was great Damages done, as I was told by the Post that comes to *Brewton*, that the Tiles of the Meeting House was blown off, and being a sort of light Tiles they flew against the Neighbouring Windows, and broke them to pieces: And at *Chalton* near *Shepton Mallet* at one. *Abbot*'s, the Roof was carried from the Walls of the House, and the House mightily shaken, and seemingly the Foundation removed, and in the Morning they found a Foundation Stone of the House upon the top of the Wall, where was a shew in the Ground of its being driven out. At *Dinder* within two Miles of *Shepton*, there was one *John Allen*, and his Son, being out of Doors in the midst of the Tempest, they saw a great Body of Fire flying on the side of a Hill, call'd *Dinder-hill*, about half a Mile from them with a Shew of black in the midst of it, and another Body of Fire following it, something smaller than the former.

There has been a strange thing at *Butly*, eight Miles from *Brewton*, which was thought to be Witchcraft, where a great many unusual Things happened to one Pope, and his Family, especially to a Boy, that was his Son, that having lain several Hours Dead, when he came to himself, he told his Father, and several of his Neighbours, strange Stories of his being carried away by some of his Neighbours that have been counted wicked Persons; the Things have been so strangely related that Thousands of People have gone to see Hand hear it; it lasted about a Year or more: But since the Storm I have inquired of the Neighbours how it was, and they tell me, that since the late Tempest of Wind the House and People have been quiet; for its generally said, that there was some Conjuration in quieting of that House. If you have a desire to hear any farther Account of it, I will make it my buiness to inquire farther of it, for there were such Things happened in that time which is seldom heard of,

Your humble Servant,

Hu. Ath.

Our Town of Butly lyes in such a place, that no Post-House is ina great many Miles of it, of you should bear oftner.

S I R,

eceived yours, desiring an Account of the Damage done by the late great Wind about us. At *Wilsnorton*, three Miles from *Wittney*, the Lead of the Church. was roused, and great Damage done to the Church, many great Elms were tore up by the Roots: At *Helford*, two Miles from us, a Rookery of Elms, was most of it tore up by the Roots: At *Cockeup*, two Miles from us, was a Barn blown down, and several Elms blown down a Cross the High-way, so that there was no passage; a great Oak of about nine or ten Loads was blown down, having a Raven sitting in it, his Wing-feathers got between two Bows, and held him fast; but the Raven received no hurt: At *Duckelton*, a little thatch'd Houte was taken off the Ground-pening, and removed a distance from the place, the covering not damaged, Hay-recks abundance are torn to pieces; At *Wittney*, six Stacks of Chimneys blown down, one House had a sheet of Lead taken from one side and blown over to the other, and many Houses were quite torn to pieces; several Hundred Trees blown down, some broke in the middle, and some torn up by the Roots. Blessed Be God: I hear neither Man, Woman nor Child that received any harm about us.

Yours Servant,
Richard Abenell.

Wittney, Oxfordsh.

ILMINSTER, Somerset

Brief but exact Remarks on the late Dreadful Storms of Wind, as it affected the Town, and the Parts adjacent.

MPRIMUS. At *Ashil*-Parish 3 Miles West from this Town, the Stable belonging to the Hare and Hounds Inn was blown down, in which were three Horses, one kill'd, another very much bruised.

2. At *Jurdans*, a Gentleman's Seat in the same Parish, there was a Brick Stable, whose Roof, one Back, and one End Wall, were all thrown down, and four foot in depth of the Fore Wall; in this Stable were 4 Horses, which by reason of the Hay-loft that bore up the Roof, were all preserv'd.

3. At *Sevington* Parish, three Miles East from this Town, *John Huthens* had the Roof of a new built House heaved clean off the Walls. *Note*, the

House was not glazed, and the Roof was thatch'd.

4. In *White Larkington* Park, a Mile East from this Town, besides four or five hundred tall Trees broken and blown down, (admirable to behold, what great Roots was turned up) there were three very large Beaches, two of them that were near five foot thick in the Stem were broken off, one of them near the Root, the other was broken off twelve Foot above, and from that Place down home to the Root was shattered and flown; the other that was not broken, cannot have less than forty Waggon Loads in it; a very fine Walk of Trees betore the House all blown down, and broke down the Roof of a Pidgeon House, the Rookery carried away in Lanes, the Lodge House damaged in the Roof, and one End by the fall of Trees. In the Garden belonging to the House, was a very fine Walk of tall Firrs, twenty of which were broken down.

5. The Damage in the Thatch of Houses, (which is the usual Covering in these Parts) is so great and general, that the price of Reed arose from twenty Shillings to fifty or three Pounds a Hundred; insomuch that to shelter themselves from the open Air, many poor People were glad to use Bean, Helm and Furse to thatch their Houses with, Things never known to be put to such Use before.

6. At *Kingston*, a Mile distance from this Town, the Church was very much shattered in its Roof, and Walls too, and all our Country Churches much shattered, so that Churches and Gentlemen's Houses which were tiled, were so shattered in their

Roofs, that at present, they are generally patch'd with Reed, not in Compliance with the Mode, but the Necessary of the Times.

7. At *Broadway*, two Miles West of this Town, *Hugh Betty*, his Wife, and four Children being in his House, it was by the violence of the Storm blown down, one of his Children killed, his Wife wounded: but recovered, the rest escaped with their Lives. A large Alms-house had most of the Tile blown off, and other Houses much shattered; a very large Brick Barn blown down, Walls and Roof to the Ground.

8. Many large Stacks of Wheat were broken, some of the Sheaves carried two or three Hundred Yards from the Place, many Stacks of Hay turned over, some Stacks of Corn heaved off the Stadle, and set down on the Ground, and not broken.

9. *Downish Walk*, two Miles South East, the Church was very much shatrered, several Load of Stones fell down, of as yet repair'd, very large Barn broken down that stood near the Church, thuch damage was done to Orchards; hot only in this Place, but in all places round, some very fine Orchards quite destroyed; some to their great Cost had the Trees set up right again, but a Storm of Wind came after, which threw down many of the Trees again; as to Timber Trees, almost all our high Trees Were broken down in that violent Storm.

10. In this Town *Henry Dunster*, his Wife and 2 Children, was in their House when it was blown down, but they all escaped with their Lives, only

one of them had a small Bruise with a piece of Timber, as the was going out of the Chamber when the Roof broke in.

The Church, in this Place, scap'd very well, as to its Roof, being cover'd with Lead only on the Chancel; the Lead was at the top of the Roof heaved up, and roll'd together, more than ten Men could turn back again, without cutting the Sheets of Lead, which was done to put it in its place again: But in general the Houses much broken and shatter'd, besides the fall of some.

This is a short, but true Account. I have heard of several other things which I have not mentioned, because I could not be positive: in the truth of them, unless I had seen it. This is what I have been to see the truth of. You may enlarge on these short Heads, and methodize them as you see good.

At *Henton St. George*, at the Lord *Pawler*'s, a new Brick Wall was broken down by the Wind for above 100 foot, the Wall being built not above 2 years since, as also above 60 Trees near 100 foot high. At *Barrington*, about 2 miles North of this Town, there was blown down aboye eight-score Trees, being of an extraordinary height, at the Lady *Strouds*.

As we shall not crowd our Relation with many Let-
ters from the same places, so it cannot he amiss
to let the World have, at least one Authentick
Account from most of those Places where any
Capital Damages havee been sustain'd, and to
summ up the rest in a general Head at the end
of this Chapter.

From Wiltshire *we have the following Account*
from the Reverend the Minister of Upper Donhead *wear* Shaftsbury; *to which the Reader is*
referr'd as follows.

S I R,

As the Undertaking you are engag'd in, to
preserve the Remembrance of the late
dreadful Tempest, is very commendable in
it self, and may in several respects be serviceable
not only to the present Age, but also to Posterity; it
merits a suitable Encouragement, and, 'tis hop'd,
it will meet with such, from all that have either a
true sense of Religion, or have had any sensible
share of the care of Providence over them, or of the
goodness of God unto them in the Land of the Living, upon that occasion. There are doubtless vast
numbers of People in all Parts (where the Tempest
raged) that have the greatest reason (as the Author
of this Paper for one hath) to bless God for their
wonderful, preservation, and to tell it to the Generation following. But to detain you no longer with

Preliminaries, I shall give you a faithful Account of what occurrd in my Neighbourhood (according to the Conditions mention'd in the Advertisement in the *Gazette*) worthy, at least, of my notice, if not of the Undertakers; and I can assure you, that the several Particulars were either such as I can vouch for on my own certain Knowledge and Observation, or else such as I am satisfy'd of the truth of by the Testimony of others, whose Integrity I have no reason to suspect. I will say no more than this in general, concerning the Storm, that, at its height, it seem'd, for some hours, to be a perfect Hurrican, the Wind raging from every Quarter, especially from all the Points of the Compass, from N. &. to the N. W. as the dismal Effects of it in these Parts do evidently demonstrate, in the demolishing of Buildings (or impairing 'em at best) and in the throwing up vast numbers of Trees by the Roots, or snapping them off in their Bodies, or larger Limbs. But as to some remarkable Particulars, you may take these following, viz.

1. The Parish-Church receiv'd little damage, tho' it stands high, the chief was in some of the Windows on the N. side, and in the fall of the Top-stone of one of the Pinnacles, which fell on a House adjoining to the Tower with little hurt to the Roof, from which glancing it rested on the Leads of the South-Isle of the Church. At the fall of ic an aged Woman living in the said House on which the Stone fell, heard horrible Scrieches (as she constantly averrs) in the Air, but none before nor after-wards.)

2. Two stone Chimney-tops were thrown down, and 2 broad Stones of each of them lay at even poize on the respective ridges of both the Houses, and tho' the Wind sat full against one of them to have thrown it off, (and then it had fallen over a Door, in and out at which several People were passing during the Storm) and tho' the other fell against the Wind, yet neither of the said Stones stirr'd.

3. A Stone of near 400 Weight, having lain about 7 Years under a Bank, defended from the Wind as it then sate, tho' it lay so long as to-be fix'd in the ground, and was as much out of the Wind, as could be, being fenced by the Bank, and a low Stone-wall up-on the Bank, none of which was demolish, tho' 2 small Holms standing in the Bank betweet the Wall, and the Scone, at the foor of the Bank were blown up by the roots; I say, this Stone, tho' thus fenced from the Storm, was carried from the place where it lay, into an hollow-way beneath, at least seven Yards from the place, where it was known to have lain for 7 Years before.

4. A Widdow-woman living in one part of an House by her self, kept her Bed till the House over her was uncover'd, and she expected the fall of the Timber and Walls; but getting below Stairs in the dark, and opening the Door to fly for shelter, the Wind was so strong in the Door, that she could neither get out at it, tho' she attempted to go out) on her knees and hands, nor could she shut the Door again with all her strength, but

was. forced to fit alone for several hours ('till the Storm slacken'd) fearing every Gust would have buried her in the Ruins; and yet it pleas'd God to preserve her, for the House (tho' a feeble one) stood over the Storm.

5. Another, who made Malt in his Barn, had been torning his Malt sometime before the Storm was at its height, and another of the Family being desirous to go again into the said Barn sometime after, was disswaded from it, and immediately thereupon the said Barn was thrown down by the Storm.

6. But a much narrower Escape had one, for whose safery the Collector of these Passages has the greatest reason to bless and praise he great Preserver of Men, who was twice in his Bed that dismal Night (tho' he had warning sufficient to deter him the first time by the falling of some of the Seiling on his Back and Shoulders, as he was preparing to go to Bed) and was altogether insensible of the great danger he was in, 'till the next morning after the Day-light appear'd, when he found the Tiles, on the side of the House opposite to the main Stress of the Weather, blown up in two places, one of which was over his Beds-head (about 9 foot above it) in which 2 or 3 Laths being broken, let down a Square of 8 or 10 Stone Tiles upon one single Lath, where they hung dropping inward a little, and bended the Lath like a Bow, but fell not: What the consequence of their Fall had been, was obvious to as many as saw it, and none has more reason to magnify God's great

Goodness, in this rescue of his Providence, than the Relater.

7. A young Man of the fame Parish, who was sent abroad to look after some black Cattle and Sheep that fed in an Inclosure, in, or near to which there were some Stacks of Corn blown down, reports, That tho' he had much difficulty to find the Inclosure in the dark, and to get thither by reason of the Tempest then raging in the height of its fury; yet being there, he saw a mighty Body of Fire on an high ridge of Hills, about 3 parts of a Mile from the said Inclosure, which gave so clear a Light into the Valley below, as that by it the said young Man could diftinctly descry all the Sheep and Cattle in the said Pasture, so as to perceive there was not one wanting.

8. At *Ashegrove*, in the same Parish (where many tall Trees were standing on the steep side of an Hill) chere were two trees of considerable bigness blown up against the side of the Hull, which seems somewhat strange, to such as have seen how many are blows, at the same place, a quite contrary way, *i. e.* down the Hill; and to fall dowswards was to fall with the Wind, as upward, was to fall against it.

9. One in this Neighbourhood had a Poplar in his Back-side of near 16 Yards high blown down, which standing near a small Current of Water, the Roots brought up near a Tun of Earth with them, and there the Tree, lay for some days after the Storm; but when the Top or Head ot the Tree; was saw'd off from the Body (tho' the Boughs were

nothing to the weight of the But End, yet) the Tree mounted, and fell back into its place, and stood as upright without its Head, as ever it had done with it. And the same happen'd at the Lady Banks her House near *Shaftsbury*, where a Wall-nut-Tree was thrown down in a place that declin'd somewhat, and after the greater Limbs had been cut off in the day time, went back in the Night following, of it self, and now stands in the same place, and posture it stood in before it was blown down. I saw it standing the 16th of this Instant, and could hardly perceive any Token or its having been Down, so very exactly it fell back into it's place. This is somewhat the more remarkable, because the Ground (as I said) 'was declining, and conquently the Tree raised against the Hill. To this I shall only add, at present, that

10. This Relator lately riding thro' a neighbouring Parish, saw two Trees near two Houses thrown besides the said Houses, and very near each House, which yet did little or no harm, when if they had fallen with he Wind, they must needs have fallen directly upon the said Houses. And

11. That this Relator had two very tall Elms thrown up by the Roots, which fell in Walnut Trees, without injuring a Twig or Bud of either of them, as rais'd the admiration of such as saw it.

12. In the same place, the Top of another Elm yet standing, was carry'd of from the Body of the Tree, a good part of 20 Yards.

S I R; I shall trouble you no further at present, you may perhaps think this enough and too much; but however that may be, you, or your ingenious Undertakers are left at liberty to publish so much, or so little of this Narrative, as shall be thought fit for the Service of the Publick. I must confess the particular Deliverances were what chiefly induced me to set Pen to Paper, tho' the other Matters are Considerable, but whatever regard you shew to the latter, in Justice you should publish the former to the World, as the Glory of God is therein concern'd more immediately, to promote which, is the only aim of this Paper. And the more effectually to induce you to do me Right, for contributing a slender Mite towards your very laudable Undertaking) I make no manner of Scruple to subscribe my self,

Sir, Yours, &c.
Rice Adams.

Upper Donhead,
Decemb. 18th 1703.

Rector of Upper-Donhead, Wilts near *Shaftsbury.*

---

*From (*Littleton *in* Worcestershire, *and* Middleton *in* Oxfordshire, *the following Letters may be a Specimen of what those whole Countries felt, and of which we have several other particular Accounts.*

S I R,

ublick notice being given of a designed Collection of the most Prodigious, as well as lamentable Effects of the last dreadful Tempest of Wind. There are many Persons hereabours, and I suppose in many other places, withall speedy furtherance and good Success to that so useful and pious Undertaking, for it may very well be thought to have a good Influence both upon the present Age, and succeeding Generation, to beget in them a holy admiration and fear of that tremendous Power and Majesty, which as one Prophet tells us, *Causeth the Vapours to ascend from the Ends of the Earth, and bringeth the Wind out of his Treasures, and as the Priest faith, bath so done his marvellous Works, that they ought to be had in remembrance.* As to these Villages of *Littleton* in *Worcestershire,* I can only give this Information, that this violent Hurricanc visited us also in its passage, to the great Terror of the Inhabitants, who although by the gracious Providence of God all escaped with their Lives and Limbs, and the main Fabrick of their Houses stood; tho' with much shaking, and some damage in the Roofs of many ot them: Yet when the Morning

Light appeared after that dismal Night, they were surpris'd with fresh apprehensions of the Dangers escaped, when they discover'd the sad Havock that was made among the Trees of their Orchards and Closes, very many Fruit Trees, and many mighty Elms being torn up, and one Elm above the rest, of very great Bulk and ancient Growth I observed, which might have defied the Strength of all the Men and Teams in the Parish, (tho' assaulted in every Branch with Roaps and Chains) was found torn up by the Roots, all sound, and of vast Strength and Thickness, and with its fall (as was thought) by the help of the same impetuous Gusts, broke off in the middle of the Timber another great Elm its Fellow, and next Neighbour. And that which may exercise the Thoughts of the Curious, some little Houses and Out-houses that seemed to stand in the same Current, and without any visible Burrough or Shelter, escaped in their Roofs, without any, or very little Damage: What Accidents of Note hapned in our Neighbouring Parishes, I suppose you may reccive from other Hands. This, (I thank God) is all that I have to transmit unto you from this place, but that I am a Well-wisher to your Work in Hand, And your Humble Servant,

Ralph Norris.

Littleton, Decem. 20.

Middleton-Stony in *Oxfordfbire,* Nov. 26. 1703.

he Wind being South West and by West, it began to blow very hard at 12 of the Clock at Night, and about four or five in the Morning Nov. 27. the Hurricane was very terrible; many large Trees were torn up by the Roots in this Place; the Leads of the Church were Roll'd up, the Stone Battlements of the Tower were blown upon the Leads, several Houses and Barns were uncover'd, part of a new built Wallof Brick, belonging to a Stable was blown down, and very much dammage, of the like Nature, was done by the Wind in the Towns and Villages adjacent.

William Offley, Rector of *Middleton-Stony.*

From Leamington Hasting, *near* Dun-*Church in* Warwickshire, *we have the following Account.*

S I R,

find in the Advertisements a Desire to have an Account of what happen'd remarkable in the late terrible Storm in the Country; the Stories every where are very many, and several of them such as will scarce gain Credit; one of them I send here an Account of being an Eye Witness, and living upon the, place: The Storm here began on the 26th of *Novem*, 1703. about 12-a-clock, but the severest Blasts were between 5 and the Morning, and between Eight and Nine the 27th I went up;to the Church, where I found all the middle Isle clearly script, of the Lead from one End to the other, and a great many of the Sheets lying on the East End upon the Church, roll'd up like a piece of Cloth: I found on the Ground six Sheets of Lead, at least 50 Hundred weight, all joyn'd together, not the least parted, but as they lay upon the Isle, which six Sheets of Lead were so carried in the Air by the Wind fifty Yards and a Foot, measured by a Workman exactly as cou'd be, from the place of the Isle where they lay, to the place they fell; and they might have been carried a great way further, had they not happen'd in their way upon a Tree, struck off an Arm of it near 17 Yards high; the End of one Sheet was twisted round the Body of the Tree, and the rest all joyn'd together lay at length, having broke down the Pales first where the Tree stood, and lay upon the Pales on the Ground, with one End of them, as I said before, round the Body of the Tree.

At the same time at *Marson*, in the County of *Warwick*, about 4 Miles from this place, a great Rick of Wheat was blown off from its Staddles, and set down without one Sheaf remov'd, or disturb'd, or without standing a-way 20 Yards from the place.

If you have a mind to be farther saisfied in this Matter, let me hear from you, and I will endeavour it: But I am in great hast at this time, which forces me to be confus'd.

I am your Friend,

E. Kingsburgh.

The following Account we have from Fareham *and* Chrift Church *in* Hampshire, *which are also well attested.*

S I R,

Ireceived yours, and in Answer these are to acquaint you; That we about us came no ways behind the rest of our Neighbours in that mighty Storm or Hurricane. As for 'our own Parish, very few Houses or Outhouses escaped. There was in the Parish of *Fareham* six Barns blown down, with divers other Outhouses, and many Trees blown up by the Roots, and other broken off in the middle; by 'the fall of a large Elm, a very large Stone Window at the West End of our Church was broken down; there was but two Stacks of Chimneys thrown down in all our Parish that I know of, and those without hurting any Person. There was in a *Coppice* called *Pupal Coppice*, an Oak Tree, of about a Load of Timber, that was twisted off with the Wind, and the Body that was left standing down to the very Roots so shivered, that if it were cut into Lengths, it would fall all in pieces. Notwithstanding so many Trees, and so much Out-Housing was blown down, I do not hear of one Beast that was killed or hurt. 'There was on the *Down* called *Portsdown*, in the Parish of *Southwick*, within three Miles of us, a Wind-Mill was blown down, that had not been up very many Years, with great damage in the said Parish to Mr. *Norton*, by the-fall of many Chimneys and Trees. The damadge sustained by using the *Healing* is such, that we are obliged to make use of Slit Deals to supply the want of Slats and Tyles until Summer come to make some. And so much Thatching wanting, that it cannot be all repaired till after another Harvest. As for Sea Affairs about us, we had but one Vessel abroad. at that time, Which was one *John Watson*, the Matter of which was never heard of yet, and I am afraid never will; I have just reason to lament her Loss, having a great deal of Goods aboard other. If at any time any particular Relation that is true, come to my knowledge in any convenient time, I will not fail to give you an Account, and at all times remain.

Your servant,
Hen. Stanton.

Fareham,
January the 23d. 170¼.

S I R,

n Answer to yours relating to the Damages done by the late Storm in, and about
our Town, is, that we had great part of
the Roof of our Church uncover'd, which was
cover'd with very large Purbick-stone, and the
Battlements of the Tower, and part of the Leads
blown down, some Stones of a vast weight blown
from the Tower, several of them between two or
three hundred weight, were blown some Rods or
Perches distance from the Church; and 12 Sheets
of Lead rouled up together, that 20 Men could not
have done the like, the great Amasement of those
that saw 'em: And several Houses and Barns low
down, with many hundreds of Trees of all sorts;
several Stacks of Chimneys being blown down,
and particularly any of one Thomas Spencer's of
this Town, who had his Top of a Brick Chimney
taken off by the House, and blown a cross a Cart
Realy and lighting upon a Barn of Richard Hollo-
way's, broke down the end of the said Barn, and
fell upright upon one End, on a Mow of Corn in
the Barn; but the said Spencer and his Wife, altho'
they were then sitting by the Fire, knew nothing
thereof until the Morning: And a Stack of Chimneys of one Mr. Imber's fell down upon a young
Gentlewoman's Bed, she having but just before
got out of the same, and several Out- houses and
Stables were blown down, some Cattel killed; and
some Wheat-ricks entirely blown off their Sta-

folds; and lighted on their bottom without any other damage; this is all the Relation I can give you that is Remarkable about us,

> *I remain your Friend and Servant*,
> William Mitchel.

At *Ringwood* and *Fording-Bridge*, several Houses and Trees are blown down, and many more Houses uncovered.

From Oxford *the following Account was sent, exclosed in the other, and are confirm'd by Letters from other Hands.*

S I R,

Inclos'd isa very exact, and I am sure, faithful Account of the Damages done by the late Violent Tempest in *Oxford*. The particulars of my Lord Bishop of *Bath* and *Wells*, and his Ladies Misfortune are as follows, The Palace is the Relicks of a very old decay'd Castle, only one Corner is new built; and had the Bishop had the good Fortune to have lain in those Apartments that Night, he had sav'd his Life. He perceivd the fall before it came, and accordingly jump't out of Bed, and made towards the Door, where he was found with his Brains dash'd out; his Lady perceiving it, wrapt all the Bed-cloaths about her, and in that manner was found smother'd in Bed. This account is Authentick,

I am, Sir, yours,
J. Bagahot.

Dec. 9. 1703.

S I R,

I give you many thanks for your account from *London*: We were no less terrified in *Oxon* with the Violence of the Storm, tho' we suffer'd in comparison but little Damage. The most considerable was, a Child kill'd in St. *Giles*'s by the fall of an House; two Pinnacles taken off from the Top of *Magdalen* Tower, one from *Merton*; about 12 Trees blown Gown in Christ Church long walk, some of the Battlements from the Body of the Cathedral, and two or three Ranges of Rails on the Top of the great Quadrangle: Part of the great Elm in University Garden was blown off, and a Branch of the Oak in *Magdalen* walks; the rest of the Colleges scaped tolerably well, and the Schools and Theatre intirely. A very remarkable passage happened at Queen's College, several Sheets of Lead judged near 6000 *l.* weight, were taken off from the Top of Sir *J. Williamson*'s Buildings, and blown against the West-end of

St. *Peter*'s Church with such Violence, that they broke an Iron-bar in the Window, making such a prodigious Noise with the fall, that some who heard it, thought the Tower had been, falling. The rest of our Losses consisted for the most part in Pinnacles, Chimneys, Trees, Slates; Tiles, Windows, &c. amounting in all, according to Computation, to not above 1000 *l.*

Ox. Dec. 7. 1703.

From Kingstone-upon-Thames, *the following Letter is very particular, and the truth of I may be depended upon.*

S I R,

I have inform'd my self of the following Matters; here was blown down a Stack of Chimneys of Mrs. Copper, Widow, which fell on the Bed, on which she lay; but the being just got up, and gone down, she rectived no harm on her Body: Likewise, here was a Stack of Chimnies of one Mr. Robert Banford's blown down, which fell on a Bed, on which his Son and Daughter lay, he was about 14 years and the Daughter 16; but they likewise were just got down Stairs, and received no harm A Stack of Chimnies at the Bull-Inn was blown down, and broke way down into the Kitchen, but hurt no Body: Here was a new Brick Malt-House of one Mr. Francis Best blown down, had not been built above two Years, blown off at the second Floor; besides many Barns, and out Houses; and very few more, some less, and Multitudes of Trees, in particular. 11 Elms of one Mr. John Bowles, Shoemaker: About 30 Apple-trees of one Mr Perce's: And of one John Andrew, a Gardiner, 100 Apple-trees blown to the Ground: One Walter Kent, Esq; had about 20 Rod of new Brick-wall of his Garden blown down: One Mr. Tiringam, Gentleman, likewise about 10 Rod of new Brick-wall blown down: Mr. George Cole, Merchant, had also some Rods of new Brick-wall blown down: Also Mr. Blitha, Merchant, had all his Walling blown down, and another extraordinary Losses. These are the most considerable Damages done here,

Your humble Servant,

C. Castleman.

From Teuxbury *in* Gloucestershire, *and from* Hatfield *in* Hartfordshire, *the following Letters are sent us from the Ministers of the respective Places.*

S I R,

ur Church, tho' a very large one, suffered no great discernable Damage. The Lead Roof, by the force of the Wind was strangely ruffled, but was laid down without any great cost or trouble. Two well-grown Elms, that stood before a sort of Alms-house in the Church-yard had a different Treatment; the one was broken short in the Trunck, and the head turn'd Southward; the other tore up by the Roots, and cast Northward: Divers Chimnies were blown down, to great Damage and Consternation of the Inhabitants: And one rising in the middle of two Chambers fell so violently, that it broke thro' the Roof and Cieling of the Chamber, and fell by the Bed of Mr. W. M. and bruised some part of the Bed teaster and Furniture; but himself, Wife and Child were signally preserved: An Out-house of Mr. F. M. (containing a Stable, Mill house, and a sort of Barn, judged about 40 Foot in length) standing at the end of our Town, and much expos'd to the Wind, intirely fell, which was the most considerable Damage: Not one of our Town and kill'd, or notably hurt; tho' fearce any but were terribly alarm'd by the dreadful Violence of it, which remitted about five in the Morning: The beautiful Cathedral Church of Glocester suffer'd much; but of that I suppose you will have an account from some proper Hand: This I was willing to signifie to you, in answer to your Letter, not that I think them worthy of a public Memorial; but the Preservation of W. M. his Wife and Child was remarkable,

Your unknown Friend
and Servant,
John Matthews.

Teuxbury *Jan.*
12. 170¼.

Bishop's Hatfield, Decem 9. *1703.*

perceive by an Advertisement in the *Gazette* of last *Monday,* that a Relation of some considerable Things which happened in the late Tempest is intended to be printed, which design I believe will be well approved of, that the Memory of it may be perpetuated. I will give you and Account of some of the observable Damages done in this Parish: The Church which was Til'd is so shattered that the Body of it is entirely to be ripp'd. Two Barns, and a Stable have been blown down; in the latter were 13 Horses, and none of them hurt, tho' there was but one to be seen when the Men first came. I have number'd about 20 large Trees blown down, which stood in the regular Walks in the Park here: It is said, that all the Trees blown down in both the Parks will make above an hundred Stacks of Wood. A Summer-house which stood on the East-side of the Bowling-green at *Hatfield*-House, was blown against the Wall, and broken, and a large part of it carried over the Wall, beyond a Cartway into the plowed Grounds. A great part of the South-wall belonging to one of the Gardens was levelled with the Ground; tho' it was so strong, that great part of it continues cemented, tho' it fell upon a Gravel-walk. Several Things which happened to incline me to think that there was something of an *Hurricane*. Part of the fine painted Glass-window in my Lord *Salisbury*'s Chapel was broken, tho' it looked towards the Fast. The North-side of an House was untiled several Yards square. In some places the Lead has been raised up, and over the Portal quite blown off. In *Brocket-hall* Park belonging to Sir *John Reade*, so many Trees are blown down, that lying as they do, they can scarce be numbered, but by a moderate Computation; they are said to amount to above a Thousand. The Damages which this Parish hath sustained, undoubtedly amount to many hundred Pounds, some of the most considerable I have mentioned to you, of which I have been in great Measure an Eye-witness, and have had the rest from Credible Persons, especially the matter of *Brocket-hall* Park, it being two Miles out of Town, tho' in this Parish. I am,

> *Sir, Your humble Servant,* George Hemsworth, *M. A. Curate of* Bishop's Hatfield, *in* Hartfordshire.

The shorter Accounts which have been sent up from almost all parts of England, *especially to the South of the* Trent; *tho' we do not transmit them at large as the abovesaid Letters are, shall be faithfully abridged for the readier comprising them within the due compass of our Volume.*

From Kent *we have many strange Accounts of the Violence of the Storm, besides what relate to the Sea Affairs.*

At Whitstable, *a small Village on the Mouth of the East Swale of the River* Medway, *we are inform'd a Boat belonging to a Hoy was taken up by the Violence of the Wind, clear off from the Water, and being bourn up in the Air, blew turning continually over and over in its progressive Motion, till it lodg'd against a rising Ground, above 50 Rod from the Water; in the passage it struck a Man, who was in the way, and broke his Knee to pieces.*

We content our selves with relating ony the Fact, and giving. Assurances of the Truth of what we Relate, we leave the needful Remarks on such Things to another place.

At a Town near Chartham, *the Lead of the Church ae up together, a blown off from the Church above* 20 *Rod distance, and being taken up afterwards, and weigh'd it, appear'd to weigh above* 2600 *weight.*

At Brenchly *in the Western Parts of* Kent, *the Spire of the Steeple which was of an extraordinary hight was overturn'd; the particulars whereof you have in the following Letter, from the Minister of the place.*

S I R,

According to your request, and my promise, for the service of the publick, I have here given you an Account of the Effects of the late Tempestuous Winds in the Parish of *Brenchly*, in the County of *Kent*, as freely and impartiality as can be consistent with the Damages sustained thereby, *viz.*

A stately Steeple, whose Altitude exceeded almost, if not all, in *Kent*, the height whereof, according to various Computations, it never in my knowledge being exactly measured, did amount at least to 10 Rods, some say 12, and others more; yet this strong and noble Structure byt he Rage of the Winds was levelled with the Ground, and made the sport and pastime of Boys and Girls, who to future Ages, tho' perhaps incredibly, yet can boast they leaped over such a Steeple, the fall ricer beardown great par of the Churchand Porch, the damage of which to repair, as before, will not amount to less than 800 or 1000 *l*. This is the publick loss; neither does private and particular much less bemoan their Condition, for some Houses, and some Barns, with other Buildings, are quite Demolished; tho' Blessed be God, not many Lives or Limbs lost in the fall, and not one House, but what suffered greatly by the Tempest. Neither were Neighbouring Parishes much more favoured; but especially, a place called *Great Peckham*, whose Steeple also, almost as high as ours, was then blown down, but not so much Damage to the Church, which God preserve safe and sound for ever.

> *This is the nearest account that can be given, by your unknown Servant,*

> Tho. Figg.

As the above Letter mentions the fall of the Spire of Great Peckham, *we have omitted a particular Letter from the place.*

In or near Hawkhurst *in* Sussex, *a Wagon standing in a Field loaden with Straw, and bound well down in order to be fetch't away the next day, the Wind took the Waggon, drove it backward into the Road, and the way being dirty, drove it with that force into the Mud or Clay of the Road, that six Horses could not pull it out.*

The Collector of these Accounts cannot but enter the Remarks he made, having occasion to Traverse the Country of Kent *about a Month after the Storm; and besides, the general Desolation which in every Village gave almost the same prospect; he declares, that he reckoned* 1107 *dwelling Houses, Out-houses and Barns blown quite down, whole Orchards of Fruit Trees laid flat upon the Ground, and of all other forts of Trees such a quantity, that tho' he attempted to take an Account of them, he found 'twas impossible, and was oblig'd to give it over.*

From Monmouth *we have a Letter, that among a vast variety of Ruins, in their own Houses and-Barns; one where of fell with a quantity of Sheep-in it, of which seven were kill'd: The Lead of the great Church, tho' on the side from the Wind, was roll'd up like a roll of Cloth, and blown off from the Church. I chose to note this, because the Letter says, it was upon the North-side of the Church, and which seems to confirm what I have observ'd before, of the Eddies of the Wind, the Operation whereof has been very strange in several Places, and more Violent than the Storm itself.*

At Wallingford, *one* Robert Dowell, *and his Wife, being both in Bed, the Chimney of the House fell in, demolish'd the House, and the main Beam breaking fell upon the Bed, the Woman receiv'd but little Damage, but the Man had his Thigh broke by the Beam, and lay in a dangerous Condition when the Letter was wrote, which was the 18th of* January *after.*

From Axminster *in* Somersetshire *take the following plain, but honest Account.*

S I R,

The best account I can give of the Storm in these Parts is as follows: Dr. *Towgood* had his Court Gate, with a piece of Wall blownto the other side of the Road, and stands upright against the Hedge, which was 12 Foot over, and it was as big as two Horses could draw a sheet of Lead which lay flat was carried from Sir *William Drake*'s quite over a Wall into the Minister's Court, near threescore Yards: There was a Tree which stood in Mr. *John Whitty*'s Ground which broke in the middle, and the top of it blew over the Hedge, and over a Wall, and over a top of a House, and did not hurt the House: There was a Mow of Corn that was blown off the Posts, and fate upright without hurt, belonging to William Oliver, at an Estate of *Edward Seymour*'s, called *Chappel Craft*: A Maiden Oke which stood in the *Quille* more than a Man could fathom, was broke in the middle: Several hundred of Apple-Trees, and other Trees blown down: Most Houses damnify'd in the Tilth and Thatch, but no Houses blown down, and no Person hurt nor killed; neither did the Church nor Tower, nor the Trees in the Church-yard received much Damage: Our loss in the Apple-Trees is the greatest; because we shall want Liquor to make our Hearts merry; the Farmer's fate them up again, but the Wind has blown them down since the Storm.

From Hartley *in the County of* Southampton, *an honest Countryman brought the following Account by way of Certificate, from the Minister of the Parish.*

S I R,

The Minister of the abovesaid Parish, in the County of *Southampton*, do hereby Certifie of the several Damages done by the late great Wind in our own, and the Parish adjacent; several dwelling Houses strip'd, and several Barns overturn'd, several Sign Posts blown down, and many Trees, both Timber and Fruit; and particularly my own Dwelling House very much mortify'd, a Chimney fell down, and endanger'd both my own, and Families Lives. I am,

Sir, your bumble Servant,
Nathan Kinsey

From Okingham *in* Berkshire, *and from* Bagshot *in* Surrey, *as follows.*

S I R,

reat damage to the Houses, some Barns down, the Market-house very much shattred, the Clock therein spoiled, several hundreds of Trees torn up by the Roots, most of them Elms, nothing more remarkablet than what was usual in other places. It is computed, that the damage amounts to 1000 *l.* And most of the Signs in the Town blown down, and some of the Leads on the Church torn up: Yet by the goodness of God, not one Person killed nor hurt.

Bagshot in *Surry.*

The Chimneys of the Mannor House, some of them blow down, and 400 Pannel of Pales, with some of the Garden Walls blown down, and in and about the Town several great Elms torn up by the Roots, most oftheHouses hatter'd, and the tops of Chimneys blown down.

In the Parish, a great many Chimneys, the tops of them blown down, and the Houses and Barns very much shatter'd, &c. the damage in all is supposed about 300 *l.* none killed.

This is all the Account I can give you concerning the damagedone by the Tempest hereabouts. This is all at present from,

Your Humble Servant,
Jo. Lewis.

Bagshot,
Feb. 1. 1704.

At Becles *the Leads of the Church ript up, part of the Great Window blown down, and the whole Town exceedingly shatter'd.*

At Ewell *by* Epsome *in* Surry, *the Lead from the flat Roof of Mr.* Williams's *House was roll'd up by the Wind, and blown from the top of the House clear over a Brick Wall near 10 Foot high, without damnifying either the House or the Wall, the Leadwas carried near 6 Rod from the House; and* as our Relator says, *was Computed toweigh near* 10 *Tun. This is Certified by Mr.* George Holdsworth *of Epsome, and sent for the Service of the present*

Collection, to the Post House at London, *to whom were refer the Truth of the Story.*

From Ely *in the County of* Cambridge, *we have the following Relation; also by a Letter from another Hand, and I the rather Transmit this Letter, because by other hands we had an account, that it was expected the Cathedral or Minster at* Ely, *being a very Antient Building, and Crasy, would not have stood the fury of the Wind, and some People that lived within the reach of it, had Terrible Apprehensions of its falling, some shocks of the Wind gave it such a Motion, that any one that felt it, would have thought it was impossible it should have stood.*

S I R,

Accoding to your request, I have made it my business to get the exactest and truest account (I am able) of the damages and losses sustain'd on this side the Country, by the late Violent Storm. The Cathedral Church of *Ely* by the Providence of God did, contrary to all Men's expectations, stand out the shock; but suffered very much in every part of it, especially that which is called the Body of it, the Lead being torn and rent up a considerable way together;

about 40 lights of Glass blown down, and shatter'd to pieces, one Ornamental Pinacle belonging to the North Isle demolish'd, and the Lead in divers other parts of it blown up into great heaps. Five Chimneys falling down in a place called the Colledge, the place where the Prebendaries Lodgings are, did no other damage (prais'd be God) then beat down some part of the Houses along with them; the loss which the Church and College of Ely sustain'd, being by computation near 2000 *l.* The Sufferers are the Reverend the Dean and Chapter of the said Cathedral. The Wind Mills belonging both to the Town and Country, felt a worse fate, being blown or burnt down by the Violence of the Wind, or else disabled to that degree, that they were wholy unable of answering the design they were made for; three of the aforesaid Mills belonging to one *Jeremiah Fouldsham* of *Ely,* a very Industrious Man of mean Substance, were burnt and blown down, to the almost Ruin and Impoverishment of the aforesaid Perfon, his particular loss being upward of a 100 *l.* these are the most remarkable disasters that beset this side of the Country. The Inhabitants both of the Town of *Ely* and Country general, receiv'd some small damages more or less in their Estates and Substance, viz. The Houses being stript of the Tiling, Barns and Out-houses laid even with the Ground, and several Stacks of Corn and Cocks of Hay being likewise much damaged, the general loss being about 20000 *l.* thee scape of all Persons here from Death, being generally miraculous; none as we can hear of being kill'd, tho' some were in more imminent danger than others. This, Sir, is as true, and as faithful an account as we are able to collect.

I am Yours,
A. Armiger.

Ely, Jan. 21. 1703.

From Sudbury *in* Suffolk, *an honest plain Countryman gives us a Letter, in which telling us of a great many Barns blown down, Trees, Chimneys and Tiles, he tells us in the Close, that their Town fared better than they expected, but that for all the neighbouring Towns they are fearfully shatter'd.*

From Tunbridge, *a Letter to the Post Master, giving the following Account.*

S I R,

cannot give you any great account of the particular damage the late great Winds has done, but at *Penchurst Park* there was above 500 Trees blown down, and the Grove at *Southborough* is almost blown down; and there is scarce a House in Town, but hath received some damage, and particularly the School House. A Stack of Chimnies blown down, but no body,God be thanked, have lost their Lives, a great many Houses have suffered very much, and several Barns have been blown down: At *East Peckam*, hard by us, the Spire of the Steeple was blown down: And at Sir *Thomas Twisden*'s in the same Parish, there was a Stable blown down, and 2 Horses killed: And at *Brenchly* the Spire of the Steeple was blown down; and at *Summer Hill Park* there were several Trees blown down; which is all at present from,

Your Servant to Command,
Elizabeth Luck.

At Laneloe *in the County of* Brecon *in Wales, a Poor Woman with a Child, was blown away by the Wind, and the Child being about 10 years old, was taken upin the Air two or three yards, and very much Wounded and Bruised in the fall.*

At Ledbury *in* Herefordshire, *we have an Acconnt of two Wind Mills blown down, and four Stacks of Chimneys in a new built Houseat a Village near* Ledbury, *which Wounded a Maid Serv-*

ant; *and at another Gentleman's House near* Ledbury, *the Coachman fearing the Stable would fall,
got his Master's Coach Horses out to save them,
but leading them by a great Stack of Hay, the
Wind blew down the Stack upon the Horses, killed
one, and Maimed the other.*

From Medhurst *in* Sussex, *the following Letter is a
short account of the loss of the Lord* Montacute,
[2]*in his Seat there, which is extraordinary great,
tho' Abridg'd in the Letter.*

S I R,

Received a Letter from you, wherein you
desire me to give you an account of what
damage was done in and about our Town,
I praise God we came off indifferent well; the
greatest damage we received, was the untiling of
Houses, and 3 Chimneys blown down, but 4 or 5
Stacks of Chimneys are blown down at my Lord
Montacute's House, within a quarter of a mile
of us, one of them fell on part of the Great Hall,
which did considerable damage; and the Church
Steeple of *Osborn*, half a mile from us, was blown
down at the same time; and my Lord had above
500 Trees torn up by the Roots, andnear us sev-

---

2   At this time, Ralph Montagu, 1st Duke of Montagu (1635 -
    1709). —Ed.

eral Barns blown down, one of Sir John Mill's, a very large Tiled Barn.

> *Your humble Servant*
> John Prinke.

Medhurst,
Jan. 18. 1704.

From Rigate *the particulars cannot be better related, than in thefollowing Letter.*

S I R,

In answer to the Letter you sent me, relating to the late great Wind, the Calamity was universal about us, great numbers of vast tall Trees were blown down, and some broken quite asunder in the middle, tho' of a very considerable bigness. Two Wind-mills were blown down, and in one there happened a remarkable Providence, and the Story thereof may perhaps be worth your observation, which is, *viz.* That the Miller of Charlewood Mill, not far from *Rigate* hearing in the night time the Wind blew very hard, arose from his Bed, and went to his Mill, resolving to turn it toward the Wind, and set it to work, as the only means to preserve it standing; but on the way feeling for the Key of the Mill, he found he had left it at his Dwelling House, and therefore returned thither to fetch it, and coming back again to the Mill, found it blown quite down, and by his lucky forgetfulness saved his Life, which otherwise he most inevitably had lost. Several Stacks of Cornand Hay were blown down and shattered a very great distance from the places where they stood. Many Barns were also blown down, and many Stacks of Chimnies; and in the Town and Parish of *Rigate*, scarce a House but suffered considerable damage, either in the Tyling or otherwise. In the Parish of *Capel* by *Darking* lived one *Charles Man*, who was in Bedwith his Wife and two Children, and by a fall of part of his House, he and one Child were killed, and his Wife, and the other Child, miraculously preserved, I am

>   *Sir, Your humble Servant,*
>   Tho. Foster.

Rigate,
Jan. 13. 170¼.

From the City of Hereford*, this Short Letter is very explicit.*

S I R,

The best account I can give of the Storm, is as follows; a Man and his Son was killed with the fall of his House, in the Parish of-

Wormsle, 2 miles off *Webly* in *Herefordfhire*. My Lord *Skudamoor*[3] had several great Oaks blown-down in the Parish of *Hom*, 4 miles from *Hereford*; there were several great Elms blown downat a place called *Hinton*, on *Wye* side, half a mile off *Hereford*, and some hundreds of Fruit Trees in other Parts of this Country, and two Stacks ofChimnies in this City, and abundance of Tiles off the old Houses,

> *Yours*, &c.
> Anne Watts.

Hereford,
Jan. 2. 1703.

At Hawkhurst, *on the Edge of* Sussex *and* Kent, *11 Barnes were blown down, besides the Houses Shatter'd or Uncover'd.*

From Basingstoke *in* Hampshire, *the following Letteris our Authority for the Particulars.*

S I R,

cannot pretend to give you a particular Account concerning the great Wind, but here are a great many Houses blown down, many Barns, and abundance of Trees. A

---

3   James Scudamore, 3rd Viscount Scudamore (1684–1716). — Ed.

little Park three Miles from *Basing Stoke*, belonging to Esq; *Waleps* has a great quantity of Timber blown down, there is 800 *l.*'s worth of Oak fold, and 800 *l.*'s worth ofother Trees to be sold, and so proportionably all over the Country. Abundance of Houses until'd,and a great many Chimneys blown down; but I donot hear of any body kill'd about us. Most of the People were in great Fearsand Consternation; insomuch, that they thought the World had been at an end. Sir,

Yours to Command W. Nevill

At *Shoram* the Market House, an Antient and very strong building, was blown flat to the Ground, and all the Town shatter'd. *Brighthelmston* being an old built and poor, tho' populous Town, was most miserably torn to pieces, and made the very Picture of Desolation, that it lookt as if an Enemy had Sackt it.

The following Letter from a small Town near Helford *in* Cornwall *is very Authentick, and may be depended on.*

S I R,

ccording to your Request, in a late Advertisement, in which you desir'd an Impartial Account of what Accidents hapned by the late Dreadful Storm, in order to make a true and just Collection of the same, please to take the following Relation, *viz.* Between 8 and 9-a-Clock the Storm began, with the Wind at N. W. about 10-a-Clock it veer'd about from W. to S. W. and back to West again, and between 11 and 12-a-Clock it blew in amost violent and dreadful manner, that the Country hereabouts thought the great day of Judgment was coming.

It continued thus blowing till 5-a-Clock, and then began to abate a little, but has done a Prodigious damage to almost all sorts of People, for either their Houses are blown down, or their Corn blown out of their Stack-yards, (some Furlongs distance) from the same, that the very Fields look in a manner, as if they had shak'd the Sheaves of Corn over them. Several Barns blown down, and the Corn that was in the same carried clear away.

The Churches here abouts have suffered very much, the Roofs of several are torn in pieces, and blown a considerable Distance off.

The small Quantity of Fruit-Trees we had in the Neighbourhood about us are so dismember'd, and torn in pieces, that few or none are left fit for bearing Fruit.

The large Timber Trees, as Elm, Oak, and the like, are generally blown down, especially the largest and highest Trees suffered most; for few Gentlemen that had Teees about their Houses have any left; and it is generally observ'd here, that the Trees and Houses that stood in Valleys, and most out of the Wind, have suffered most. In short, the Damage has been so general, that both Rich and Poor have suffered much.

In *Helford*, a small Haven, not far from hence, there was a Tin Ship blown from her Anchors with only one Man, and two Boys on Board, without Anchor, Cable or Boat, and was forc'd out of the said Haven about 12-a Clock at Night; the next Morning by 8-a Clock, the Ship miraculously Run in between two Rocks in the *Isle of Wight,* where the Men and Goods were saved, but the Ship lost: Such a Run, info short a time, is almost Incredible, it being near 80 Leagues in 8 hours time, I believ-eit to be very true, for the Master of the said Ship I know very well, and some that were concern'd in her Lading, which was Tin, &c.

From St. Keaverne *Parish in* Cornwall,
Yours &c. W. T.

May 26.1704.

Thus far our Letters.

It has been impossible to give an exact relation in the matter of publick Damage, either as to the particulars of what is remarkeable, or an Estimate of the general loss. The Abstract here given, as near as we could order it, is so well taker, that we have, *generally speaking,* something remarkable from everyquarter of the Kingdom, to the South of the *Trent.*

It has been observ'd, that tho' it blew a great Storm farther Northward, yet nothing so furious as this way. At *Hull,* indeed, as the Relation Expresses, it was violent, but even that violence was moderate, compar'd to the Stupendious fury with which all the Southern part of the Nation was Attack'd.

When the Reader finds an Account here from *Milford-haven* in Wales, and from *Helford* in *Cornwall* West, from *Yarmouth* and *Deal* in the East, from Portsmouth in the South, and *Hull* in the North, I am not to imagine him so weak as to suppose all the vast Interval had not the same, or proportion'd suffering, when you find one Letter from a Town, and two from a County, it is not to be supposed that was the whole damage in that County, but, on the contrary, that every Town in the County suffered the same thing in proportion; and it would have been endless to the Collector, and tiresom to the Reader, to have Enumerated all the Individuals of every County; 'twould be endless to tell the the Desolation in the Parks, Groves, and fine Walks of the Gentry, the general havock in the Orchards and Gardens among the Fruit Trees, especially in the Countries of *Devon, Somerset, Hereford, Gloucester* and *Worcester,* where the making great quantities of Cyder and Perry, is the reason of numerous and large Orchards, among which, for several Miles together, there would be very few Trees left.

In *Kent* the Editor of this Book has seen several great Orchards, the Trees lying flat on the

Ground, and perhaps one Tree standing in a place by it self, as a House might shelter it, perhaps none at all.

So many Trees were every where blown crots the Road, that till the People were call'd to saw them off, and remove them, the ways were not passable.

Stacks of Corn and Hay were in all places either blown down, or so torn, that they receiv'd great damage, and in this Article 'tis very observable, those which were only blown down receiv'd the least Injury; when the main body of a Stack of Hay stoodsafe, thetop being loosen'd by the Violence of the Wind, the Hay was driven up into the Air, and flew about like Feathers, that it was entirely lost, and hung about in the Neighbouring Trees, and spread on the Ground for a great distance, and so perfectly seperated, that there was no gathering it together.

Barly and Oats suffered the same casualty, only that the weight of the Cornfettled it sooner to the Ground than the Hay.

As to the Stacks of Wheat, the Accounts are very strange; from many places we have Letters, and some so incredible, that we dare not venture on the Readers faith to transmit them, least they should shock their belief in those very strange Relations already set down, and better Attested, as of a great Stack of Corn taken from the Hovel on which it stood, and without Dislocating the Sheaves, set up another Hovel, from whence the Wind had just before remov'd another Stack of equal Dimensions; of a Stackof Wheat taken up with the Wind, and set down whole 16 Rod off, and the like. But as we have other Relations equally strange, their Truth considered, we refer the Reader to them, and assure the World we have several Accounts of Stacks of Wheat taken clear off from the Frame or Steddal, and set down whole, abundance more over-set, and thrown off from their standings, and others quite dispers'd, and in a great measure destroy'd.

'Tis true, Corn was exceeding cheap all the Winter after, but they who bring that as a reason to prove there was no great quantity destroy'd, are oblig'd to bear with me in telling them they are mistaken, for the true reason was as follows,

The Stacks of Corn in some Countries, the West chiefly, where the People generally lay up their Corn in Stacks, being so damnify'd as above, and the Barns in all parts being Universally uncovered, and a vast number of them overturn'd, and blown down, the Country People were under a necessity of Threshing out their Corn with all possible speed, least if a Rain had follow'd, as at that time of Year was not unlikely, it might ha' been all spoil'd.

And it was a special Providence to those People also, as well as to us in *London*, that it did not Rain, at least to any quantity, for near three Weeks after the Storm.

Besides this, the Country People were obliged to thresh out their Corn for the sake of the Straw, which they wanted to repair the Thatch, and covering of their Barns, in order to secure the rest.

All these Circumstances forc'd the Corn to Market in unusual quantities, and that by Consequence made it Cheaper than ordinary, and not the exceeding quantity then in Store.

The Seats of the Gentlemen in all places had an extraordinary share in the Damage; their

Parks were in many places perfectly disman- tled, the Trees before their Doors levelled, their Garden Walls blown down, and I could give a Lift, I believe, of a thousand Seats in England, within the compass of our Collected Papers, who had from 5 to 20 Stacks of Chimnies blown down, some more, some less, according to the several Dimentions of the Houses.

I am not obliging the Readerto comply with the Calculations here following, and it would have took up too much room in this small Tract to name particulars; but according to the best estimate I have been able to make from the general Accounts sent up by Persons forward to have this matter recorded, the following particulars are rather under than over the real Truth.

25 Parks in the several Countries, who have above 1000 Trees in each Park, blown down.

New Forest in *Hampshire* above 4000, and some of prodigious Bigness; above 450 Park- sand Groves, who have from 200 large Trees to 1000 blown down in them.

Above 100 Churches covered with Lead, the Lead roll'd up, the Churches uncover'd; and on some of them, the, Lead in prodigious Quan- tities blown to incredible Distances from the Church.

Above 400 Wind-mills overset, and broken to pieces; or the Sails so blown round, that the Timbers and Wheels have heat and set the rest on Fire, and so burnt them down, as particular- ly several were in the Isle of *Ely*.

Seven Steeples quite blown down, besides abundance of Pinacles and Battlements from those which stood; and the Churches where it happened most of them Demolish'd, or terribly Shattered.

Above 800 dwelling Houses blown down, in most of which the Inhabitants received some Bruise or Wounds, and many lost their Lives.

We have reckoned, including the City of *London*, about 123 People kill'd; besides such as we have had no account of; the Number of People drowned are not easily Guest; but by all the Calculations I have made and seen made, we are within compass, if we reckon 8000 Men lost, includingwhat were lost on the Coast of *Holland*, what in Ships blown away, and never heard of, and what were drowned in the Flood of the Severn, and in the River of *Thames*.

What the Loss, how many poor Families ruin'd, is not to be Estimated, the Fire of *London* was an exceeding Loss, and was by some reckon'd at four Millions sterling; which, tho' it was a great Loss, and happened upon the spot,where vast Quantities of Goods being expos'd to the fury of the Flames,were destroy'd in a hurry,and 14000 & dwelling Houses entirely consum'd.

Yet on the other Hand, that Desolation was confin'd to a small Space, the loss fell on the wealthiest part of the People; but this loss is Universal, and its extent general, not a House, not a Family that had any thing to lose, but have lost something by this Storm, the Sea, the Land, the Houses, the Churches, the Corn, the Trees, the Rivers, all have felt the fury of the Winds.

I cannot therefore think I speak too large, if I say, I am of the Opinion, that the Damage done by this Tempest far exceeded the Fire of *London*.

They tell us the Damages done by the Tide, on the Banks of the *Severn*, amounts to above 200000 pounds, 15000 Sheep drown'd in one Level, Multitudes of Cattle on all the sides, and the covering the Lands with Salt Water is a Damage cannot well be Estimated: The High Tide at *Bristol* spoil'd or damnify'd 1500 Hogsheds of Sugars and Tobaccoes, besides great quantities of other Goods.

'Tis impossible to describe the general Calamity, and the most we can do is, to lead our Reader to supply by his Immagination what we omit; and to believe, that as the Head of the particulars is thus collected, an of infinite Variety at the same time happened in every place, which cannot be expected to be found in this Relation.

There are some additional Remarks to be made as to this Tempests, which I cannot think improper to come in here: As,

1. That in some Parts of *England* it was join'd with terrible Lightnings and Flashings of Fire, and in other Places none at all, as to Thunder-the Noise the Wind made, was so Terrible, and so Unusual, that I will not say, People might not mistake it for Thunder; but I have not met with any, who will be positive that they heard it Thunder.

2. Others, as in many Letters we have received to that purpose insist upon it, that they felt an Earthquake; and this I am doubtful offor several Reasons.

1st. We find few People either in City or Country ventur'd out of their Houses, or at least till they were forced out, and I cannot find any Voucher to this opinion of an Earthquake, from those whose Feet stood upon the *Terra Firma*, felt it move, and will affirm it to be so.

2d. As to all those People who were in Houses, I cannot allow them to be competent Judges, for as no House was so strong as not to moveand shake with the force of the Wind, so it must be impossible for them to distinguish whither that motion came from above or below: As to those in Ships, they will not pretend to be competent Judges in this case, and I think the People within doors as improper to decide, for what might not that motion they felt in their Houses, from the Wind do, that an Earthquake could do. We found it rockt the strongest Buildings, and in several places made the Bells in the Steeples strike, loosen'd the Foundations of the Houses, and in some blew them quitedown, but still if it had been an Earthquake, it must have been felt in every house, and every place; and whereas in those Streets of *London*, where the Houses stand thick and well Built, they could not be so shaken with the Wind as in opener places; yet there the other would have equally been felt, and better distinguisht; and this particularly by the Watch, who stood on the Ground, under shelter of publick Buildings, as in St. Paul's Church, the Exchange Gates, the Gates of the City, and such like; wherefore, as I am not for handing to Posterity any matter of Fact upon ill Evidence, soI cannot transmit what has its Foundation only in the Amazements of the People.

'Tis true, that there was an Earthquake felt in the *North East parts of the Kingdoms*, about a Month afterwards, of which several Letters here

inferted make mention, and one very particularly from *Hull*; but that there was any such thing as
an Earthquake during the Storm, I cannot agree.

Another remarkable thing I have observ'd,
and have several Letters to show of the Water
which fell in the Storm, being brackish, and at
Cranbrook in *Kent*, which is at least 16 Miles
from the Sea, and above 25 from any Part of the
Sea to windward, from whence the Wind could
bring any moisture, *for it could not be suppos'd
to fly against the Wind*; the Grass was so salt,
the Cattel would not eat for several Days, from
whence the ignorant People suggested another
Miracle, *viz.* that it rain'd salt Water.

The answer to this, I leave to two Letters printed
in the *Philosophical Transactions*; as follows,

Part of a Letter from Mr. Denham *to the Royal
Society,*

S I R,

have just now, since my writing, receiv'd an
account from a Clergy-man, an Intelligent
Person at *Lewes* in *Sussex*, not only that
the Storm made great desolations there abouts,
but also an odd Phænomenon occasioned by it, *viz.*

That a Physician travelling soon after the Storm
to *Tisehyrst*, about 20 Miles from *Lewes*, and as

far from the Sea, as he rode he pluckt some tops of Hedges, and chawing them found them Salt. Some Ladies of *Lewes* hearing this, tasted some Grapes that were still on the Vines, and they also had the same relish. The Grass on the Downs in his Parish was so salt, that the Sheep in the Morning would not feed till hunger compelled them, and afterwards drank like Fishes, as the Shepherds report. This he attributeth to Saline Particles driven from the Sea.——He heareth also, that People about *Portsmouth* were much annoyed with sulphurous Fumes, complaining they were most suffocated therewith.

V. *Part of a Letter from Mr.* Anthony van Lauwenhoek, *F. R. S. giving his Observations on the late Storm.*

Delft, Jan. 8. 1704. N. S.

S I R,

Affirmed in my Letter of the 3d of November last past, that Water may be so dash'd and beaten against the Banks and Dikes by a strong Wind, and divided into such small Particles, as to be carried far up into the Land.

Upon the 8th of December, 1703. N. S. We had a dreadful Storm from the South West, insomuch, that the Water mingled with small parts of Chalk and Stone, was so dasht against the Glass-windows, that many of them were darkned therewith, and the lower Windows of my House, which are made of very fine Glass, and always kept well scower'd, and were not open'd till 8-a-Clock that Morning, notwithstanding that they look to the North East, and consequently food from the Wind; and moreover, were guarded from the Rain by a kind of Shelf or Pent-house over them; were yet so cover'd with the Particles of the Water which the Whirl-wind cast against them, that in less than half an hour they were deprived of most of their transparency, and, forasmuch as these Particles of Water were not quite exhaled, I concluded that it must be Sea-water, which the said Storm had not only dasht against our Windows, but spread also over the whole Country.

That I might be satisfied herein, I blow'd two small Glasses, such as I thought most proper to make my Observations with, concerning the Particles of Water that adhered to my Windows.

Pressing these Glasses gently against my Windows, that were covered with the suppos'd Particles of Sea-water, my Glasses were tinged with a few of the said Particles.

These Glasses, with the Water I had thus collected on them, I placed at about half a Foot distance from the Candle, I view'd them by my Microscope, reck'ning, that by the warmth of the Candle, and my Face together, the Particles of the said Water would be put into such a motion, that they would exhale for the most part, and the

Salts that were in 'em would be expos'd naked to the fight, and so it happened; for in a little time a great many Salt Particles did, as it were, come out of the Water, having the Figure of our common Salt, but very small, because the Water was little, from whence those small Particles proceeded; and where the Water had lain very thin upon the Glass, there were indeed a great number of Salt Particles, but so exceeding fine, that they almost escaped the Sight through a very good Microscope.

From whence I concluded, that these Glass windows could not be brought to their former Lustre, but by washing them with a great deal of Water; for if the Air were very clear, and the Weather dry, the watry Particles would soon exhale, but the Salts would cleave fast to the Glass, which said Salts would be again dissolv'd in moist Weather, and sit like a Dew or Mist upon the Windows.

And accordingly my People found it when they came to wash the aforementioned lower Windows of my House; but as to the upper Windows, where the Rain had beat against them, there was little or no Salt to be found sticking upon that Glass.

Now, if we consider, what a quantity of Sea-water is spread all over the Country by such a terrible Storm, and consequently, how greatly impregnated the Air is with the same; we ought not to wonder, that such a quantity of Water, being moved with so great a force, should do so much mischief to Chimneys, tops of Houses, &c. not to mention the Damages at Sea.

During the said Storm, and about 8-a-Clock in the Morning, I cast my Eye upon my Barometer, and observ'd, that I had never seen the Quick-silver so low; but half an hour after the Quick-silver began to rise, tho' the Storm was not at all abated, at least to any appearance; from whence I concluded, and said it to those that were about me, that the Storm would not last long; and so it happened.

There are some that affirm, that the scattering of this Salt-water by the Storm will do a great deal of harm to the Fruits of the Earth; but for but for my part I am of a quite different Opinion, for I believe that a little Salt Spread over the surface of the Earth, especially where it is heavy Clay-ground, does render it exceeding Fruitful; and so it would be, if the Sand out of the Sea were made use of to the same purpose

---

These Letters are too well, and too judiciously Written to need any comment of mine; 'tis plain, the watry Particles taken up from the Sprye of the Sea into the Air, might by the impetuosity of the Winds be carried a great way, and if it had been much farther, it would have been no Miracle in my account; and this is the reason, why I have not related these Things, among the extraordinary Articles of the Storm.

That the Air was full of Meoters, and fiery Vapours, and that the extraordinary Motion occasion'd the firing more of them than usual, a small stock of Philosophy will make very rational; and of these we have various Accounts, more

in some places than in others, and I am apt to believe these were the Lighntings we have been told of; for I am of Opinion, that there was really no Lightning, such as we call so in the common Acceptation of it; for the Clouds that flew with so much Violence through the Air, were not, as to my Observation, such as usually are fraighted with Thunder and Lightning, the Hurries nature was then in, do not consist with the System of Thunder, which is Air pent in between the Clouds; and as for the Clouds that were seen here flying in the Air, they were by the fury of the Winds so seperated,and in such small Bodies, that there was on room for a Collection suitable,and necessary to the Case we speak of.

These Cautions I thought necessary to set down here, for the satisfaction of the Curious; andas they are only my Opinions, I submit them to the judgment of the Reader.

Of the Damages on the Water

s this might consist of several Parts, I was inclin'd to have divided it into Sections or Chapters, relating particularly to the publick Loss, and the private; to the Merchant, or the Navy, to Floods by the Tides, to the River Damage, and that of the Sea; but for brevity, I shall confine it to the following particulars.

First, *The Damage to Trade.*
Secondly, *The Damage to the Royal Navy.*
Thirdly, *The Damage by High Tides.*

First, *Of the Damage to Trade.*

I might call it a Damage to Trade, that this Season was both for some time before and after the Tempest, so exceeding, and so continually Stormy, that the Seas were in a manner Unnavigable and Negoce, at a kind of a general Stop, and when the Storm was over, and the Weather began to be tolerable; almost all the Shipping in *England* was more or less out of Repair, for there was very little Shipping in the Nation, but what had receiv'd some Damage or other.

It is impossible, but a Nation so full of Shipping as this, must be exceeding Sufferers in such a general Disaster, and who ever considers the Violence of this Storm by its other dreadful Effects will rather wonder, and be thankful that we receiv'd no farther Damage, than we shall be able to give an Account of by Sea.

I have already observ'd what Fleets were in the several Ports of this Nation, and from whence they came: As to Ships lost of whom we have no other Account than that they were never heard of. I am not able to give any Perticulars, other than that about three and forty Sail of all Sorts are reckon'd to have perished in that manner. I mean of such Ships as were at Sea, when the Storm began, and had no Shelter or Port to make for their Safety: Of these, some were of the Russia Fleet, of whom we had an Account of 20 Sail lost the Week before the great Storm, but most of them reach'd the Ports of *Newcastle*, *Humber* and *Yarmouth*, and some of the Men suffered in the general Distress afterwards.

But to proceed to the most general Disasters, by the same Method, as in the former Articles of Damages by Land. Several Person shaving given themselves the Trouble to further this Design with Authentick Particulars from the respective Ports. I conceive we cannot give the World a clearer and more Satisfactory Relation than from their own Words.

The first Account, and plac'd so, because 'tis very Authentick and Particular, and the furthest Port Westward, and therefore proper to begin our Relation, is from on Board her Majesty's Ship the Dolphin *in* Milford Haven, *and sent to us by Capt* Soanes *the Commodore of a Squadron of Men of War the ninth at Harbour, to whom the Public is very much oblig'd for the Relation, and which we thought our selves bound there to acknowledge. The Account is as follows,*

S I R,

Reading the Advertisement in the *Gazette*, of your intending to Print the many sad Accidents in the late dreadful Storm, induced me to let you know what this place felt, tho' a very good Harbour. Her Majesty's. Ships the *Cumberland*, Coventry, Loo, Hastings and Hector, being under my Command, with the *Rye* a Cruizer on this Station, and under our Convoy about 130 Merchant Ships bound about Land;

168

the 26th of November at one in the Afternoon the
Wind came at S. by E. a hard Gale, between which
and N.W. by W. it came to a dreadful Storm, at
three the next Morning was the Violente t of the
Weather, when the *Cumberland* broak her Sheet
Anchor, the Ship driving near this, and the Rye,
both narrowly escap'd carrying away; she drove
very near the Rocks, having but one Anchor left,
but in a little time they flung a Gun, with the
broken Anchor fast to it, which they let go, and
wonderfully preserv'd the Ship from the Shoar.
Guns firing from one Ship or other all the Night
for help,tho' 'twas impossible to assist each other, the Sea was so high, and the Darkness of the
Night such, that we could not see where anyone
was, but by the Flashes of the Guns; when day-
light appear'd, it was a dismal sight to behold the
Ships driving up and down one foul of another,
without Masts, some sunk, and others upon the
Rocks, the Wind blowing so hard, with Thunder,
Lightning and Rain, that on the Deck a Man could
not stand without holding. Somedrove from Dale,
where they were shelter'd under the Land, and
split in pieces, the Men all drowned; two others
drove out of a Creek, one on the Shoar so highup
was saved, the other on the Rocks in another
Creek, and Bulg'd; an Irish Ship that lay with a
Rock thro' her, was lifted by the Sea clear away
to the otherside of the Creek on a safe place; one
Ship forc'd 10 Miles up the River before she could
be stop'd, and several strangely blown into holes,

and on Banks; a Ketch of *Pembroke* was drove on the Rocks, the two Men and a Boy in her had no Boat to save their Lives; but in this great distress a Boat which broke from another Ship drove by them, without any in her, the two Men leap into her, and were sav'd, but the Boy drown'd; a Prize at Pembroke was lifted on the Bridge, whereon is a Mill, which the Water blew up, but the Vessel got off again; another Vessel carried almost into the Gateway which leads to the Bridge, and is a Road, the Tide flowing several Foot above its common Course. The Storm continu'd till the 27th about 3 in the Afternoon; that by Computation nigh 30 Merchant Ships and Vessels without Masts are lost, and what Menare lost is not known; 3. Ships are missing, that we suppose Men and all lost. None of her Majesty's Ships cameto any harm; but the *Cumberland* breaking her Anchor in a Storm which happen'd the 18th at Night, lost another, which renders her uncacapable of proceeding with us till supply'd. I saw several Trees and Houses which are blown down.

Your Humble Servant,
Jos. Soanes.

The next Accountwe have from the Reverend Mr. Tho. Chest, Minister of Chepstow, whose Ingenious account being given in his own Words, gives the best Acknowledgement for his forwarding and approving this design.

S I R,

pon the Evening of *Friday, Nov. 26. 1703.* the Wind was very high; but about midnight it broke out with a more than wonted Violence, and so continued till near break of day. It ended a N. W. Wind, tho' about 3 in the Morning it was at S. W. The loudest cracks I observed of it, were some what before 4 of the Clock; we had here the common Calamity of Houses shatter'd and Trees thrown down.

But the Wind throwing the Tyde very strongly into the *Severn*, and so into the Wye, on which *Chepstow* is scituated. And the Freih in *Wye* meeting with a Rampant Tyde, over flowed the lower part of our Town. It came into several Houses about 4 foot high, rather more; the greatest damage sustained in Houses, was by the makers of Salt, perhaps their loss might amount to near 200 *l.*

But the Bridge was a strange sight; it stands partly in *Monmouthshire*, and partly in *Gloucestershire*, and is built mostly of Wood, with a Stone Peer in the midst, the Center of which divides the two Counties; there are also Stone Platforms in the bottom of the River to bear the Wood-work. I doubt not but those Stone Platforms were covered then by the great Fresh that came down the River. But over these there are Wooden Standards fram'd into Peers 42 Foot high; besides Groundsils, Cap-heads, Sleepers, Planks, and (on each side of the Bridge) Rails which may make about 6 foot more, the Tyde came over them all: The length of the Wooden part of the Bridge in *Monmouthshire* is 60 yards exactly, and thereabout in Gloucestershire; the *Gloucestershire* side suffered but little, but in *Monmouthshire* side the Planks were most of them carried away, the Sleepers (about a Tun by measure each) were many of them carried away, and several removed, and 'tis not doubted but the Wooden Peers would have gone too; great but it was so, that the outward Sleepers on each side the Bridge were Pinn'd or Bolted to the Cap heads, and so kept them in their places.

All the level Land on the South part of *Monmouthshire*, called the Moors, was overflow'd; it is a tract of Land about 20 miles long, all Level, save 2 little points of High-land, or 3; the Breadth of it is not all of one size, the broadest part is about 2 miles and ½. Tyde came 5 Tydes before the top of the Spring, according to the usual run, which surprized the People very much. Many of their Cattle got to shore, and some dy'd after they were landed. It is thought by a *Moderate Computation*, they might lose in Hay and Cattle between 3 and 4000 *l.* I cannot hear of any Person drowned, save only one Servant Man, that ventur'd in quest of his

Master's Cattle. The People were carried off, some by Boats, some other ways, the days following; the last that came off (that I can hear of) were on *Tuesday* Evening, to be sure they were uneasy and astonished in that Interval. There are various reports about the height of this Tyde in the *Moors*, comparing it with that in Jan. 1606. But the account that seems likeliest to me, is, that the former Tyde ran some what higher than this. 'Tis thought most of their Land will be worth but little these 2 or 3 years, and 'tis known, that the repairing the Sea Walls will be very chargeable.

Gloucestershire too, that borders upon *Severne* hath suffered deeply on the Forrest of *Deane* side, but nothing in comparison of the other shore, from about *Harlingham* down to the mouth of *Bristol* River *Avon*, particularly from *Aust Cliffe* to the Rivers Mouth (about 8 miles) all that Flat, called the Marsh was drowned. They lost many Sheep and Cattle. About 70 Seamen were drown'd out of the *Canterbury* Storeship, and other Ships that were Stranded or Wreck'd. The Arundel Man of War, *Suffolk* and *Canterbury* Storeships, a *French* Prize, and a *Dane*, were driven ashore and damnified; but the *Arundel* and the *Danish* Ship are got off, the rest remain on Ground. The *Richard and John* of about 500 Tun, newly come into King-road from *Virginia*, was Staved. The *Shoram* rode it out in King-road; but I suppose you may have a perfecter account of these things from *Bristol*. But one thing yet is to be remem bred, one *Nelms* of that Country, as I hear his Name, was carried away with his Wife and 4 Children, and House and all, and were all lost, save only one Girl, who caught hold of a Bough, and was preserved.

There was another unfortunate Accident yet in these parts, one Mr. *Churchman*, that keeps the Inns at *Betesley*, a passage over the *Severn*, and had a share in the passing Boats, seeing a single Man tossed in a Wood-buss off in the River, prevailed with some belonging to the Customs, to carry himself and one of his Sons, and 2 Servants aboard the Boat, which they did, and the Officers desired Mr. *Churchman* to take out the Man, and come ashore with them in their Pinnace. But he, willing to save the Boat as well as the Man, tarried aboard, and sometime after hoisting Sail, the Boat overset, and they were all drowned, *viz.* the Man in the Boat, Mr. *Churchman*, his Son and 2 Servants, and much lamented, especially Mr. *Churchman*, and his Son, who were Persons very useful in their Neighbourhood. This happened on Saturday about 11 of the Clock.

Your Humble Servant,
Tho. Chest.

Mr. Tho. Little Minister of —————— *Church in Lyn, in the County of* Norfolk, *being request-ed to give in the particulars of what happen'd thereabouts, gave the following, short, but very pertinent Account.*

S I R,

I had answer'd yours sooner, but that I was willing to get the best Information I could of the effect of the late dismal Storm amongst us. I have advis'd with our Merchants, and Ship Masters, and find that we have lost from this Port 7 Ships, the damage whereof, at a modest Compu-tation, amounts to 3000 *l.* the Men that perish'd in them are reckon'd about 20 in number. There is another Ship missing, tho' we are not without hopes that the is gone Northward, the value of Ship and Cargo about 1500 *l.*

The Damage sustain'd in the Buildings of the Town is computed at 1000 *l.* at least.

I am your faithful Friend and Servant.
Tho. Little

Lyn, Jan. 17. 1703.

We have had various Accounts from Bristol, but as they all contain something of the same in general, only differently Exprest, the following, as the most possitively asserted, and best Exprest, is recorded for the publick Information.

S I R,

bserving your desire (lately signify'd in the *Gazette*) to be further inform'd concerning the Effects of the late dreadful Tempest, in order to make a Collection thereof. I have prefum'd to present you with the following particulars concerning *Bristol*, and the parts near Adjacent, being an Eye-witness of the same, or the Majority of it. On *Saturday* the 27th of *Novemb.* last, between the hours of one and two in the Morning, arose amost prodigious Storm of Wind, which continued with very little intermission for the space of 6 hours, in which time it very much shattered the Buildings, both publick and private, by uncovering the Houses, throwing down the Chimneys, breaking the Glass Windows, overthrowing the Pinnacles and Battlements of the Churches, and blowing off the Leads: The Churches in particular felt the fury of the Storm. St. *Stephen*'s Towerhad three Pinnacles blown off, which beat down the greatest part of the Church. The Cathedral is likewise very much defac'd, two of its Windows, and several Battlements being blown away; and, indeed, most Churches in the City felt its force more or less; it also blew down abundance of great Trees in the Marsh, *College-Green*, St. *James*'s Church-yard, and other places in the City. And in the Country it blew down and scattered abundance of Hay and Corn Mows, besides almost Levelling many Orchards and Groves of stout Trees. But the greatest damage done to the City was, the violent over-flowing of the Tide, occasion'd by the force of the Wind, which flowed an extraordinary height, and did abundance of damage to the Merchants Cellers. It broke in with great fury over the Marsh Country, forcing down the Banks or Sea Walls, drowning abundance of Sheep, and other Cattle, washing some houses clear away, and breaking down part of others, in which many Persons lost their Lives. It likewise drove most of the Ships in *Kingroad* a considerable way upon the Land, some being much shatter'd, and one large Vessel broke all in pieces, and near all the Men lost, besides several lost out of other Vessels. To conclude, the Damage sustein'd by this City alone in Merchandise, Computed to an Hundred Thousand Pounds, besides the great Loss in the Country, of Cattel, Gorn, &c. which has utterly ruined many Farmers, whose substance consisted in their Stock aforesaid. So having given you the most material Circumstances, and fatal Effects of this great Tempest in these Parts. I conclude

Your (unknown) Friend and Servant,
Danial James.

From Huntspill *in* Somersetshire, *we have the following Account from, as we suppose, the Minister of the place, tho' unknown to the Colletor of this Work.*

S I R,

The Parish of *Huntspill* hath receiv'd great Damage by the late Inundation of the Salt Water, particularly the West part thereof suffered most: For on the 27th Day of *November* last, about four of the Clock in the Morning, a mighty Southwest Wind blew so strong, as (in a little time) strangely tore our Sea Walls; insomuch, that a considerable part of the said Walls were laid smooth, after which the Sea coming in with great Violence, drove in five Vessels belonging to *Bridgewater* Key out of the Channel, upon a Wharf in our Parish, which lay some distance off from the Channel, and there they were all grounded; it is said, that the Seamen there fathom'd the depth, and found it about nine Foot, which is taken notice to be four Foot above our Walls when standing; the Salt Water soon overflow'd all the West end of the Parish, forcing many of the Inhabitants from their Dwellings, and to shift for their Lives: The Water threw down several Houses, and in one an antient Woman was drown'd, being about fourscore Years old: Some Families shelter'd themselves in the Church, and there staid till the Waters were abated: Three Window Leaves of the

Tower were blown down, and the Ruff-cast scal'd off in many places: Much of the Lead of the Church was damnify'd; the Windows of the Church and Chancel much broken, and the Chancel a great part of it untiled: The Parsonage House, Barn and Walls received great Damage; as also, did some of the Neighbours in their Houses: At the West end of the Parsonage House stood a very large Elm, which was four Yards a quarter and half a quarter in the Circumference, it was broken off near the Ground by the Wind, without forcing any one of the Moars above the Surface, but remain'd as they were before: The Inhabitants (many of them) have receiv'd great Losses in their Sheep, and their other Cattle; in their Corn and Hay there is great spoil made. This is what Information I can give of the Damage this Parish hath sustain'd by the late dreadful Tempest.

> *I am, Sir,*
> > *Your humble Servant,*
> > > Sam. VVooddelon.

Huntspill,
January 6. 170¼

From Minehead *in* Somersetshire, *and* Swanzy *in* Wales, *the following Accounts are to be depended upon.*

S I R,

I received yours, and in answer to it these are to acquaint you, that all the Ships in our Harbour except two (which were 23 or 24 in Number, besides Fishing Boats) were, through the Violence of the Storm, and the mooring Posts giving way, drove from their Anchors, one of them was stav'd to pieces, nine drove Ashoar; but 'tis hoped will be all got off again, though some of them are very much damnified: Several of the Fishing Boats likewise, with their Nets, and other Necessaries were destroy'd. Three Seamen were drowned in the Storm, and one Man was squeez'd to Death last Wednesday, by one of the Ships that was forc'd Ashoar, suddenly coming upon him, as they were digging round her, endeavouring to get her off.

Our Peer also was somewhat damaged, and 'tis thought, if the Storm had continued till another Tide, it would have been quite washed away, even level to the Ground; which if so, would infallibly have ruined our Harbour: Our Church likewise was almost all untiled, the neighbouring Churches also received much Damage: The Houses of our Town, and all the Country round about, were most of them damaged; some (as I am credibly informed) blown down, and several in a great Measure uncovered: Trees also of a very great Bigness were broken off in the middle, and vast Numbers blown down; one Gentleman, as he told me himself, having 2500 Trees blown down: I wish you good Success in these your Undertakings, and I pray God that this late great Calamity which was sent upon us as a punishment for our Sins, may be a warning to the whole Nation in general, and engage every one of us to a hearty and sincere Repentance; otherwise, I'm afraid we must expect greater Evils than this was to fall upon us.

From your unknown Friend and Servant,
Frist. Chave.

Swanzy, January 24, 1704/4.

S I R,

I receiv'd yours and accordingly have made an enquiry in our Neighbourhood: what damage might be done in the late Storm, thro' Mercy we escap'd indifferently, but you will find underwritten as much as I can learn to be certainly true.

The Storm began here about 12 at Night, but the most violent part of it was about 4 the next Morning, about which time the greatest part of the Houses in the Town were uncovered more or less, and one House clearly blown down; the damage sustain'd to the Houses is modestly computed at 200 *l.* the South Isle of the Church was wholly uncovered, and considerable damage done to the other Isles, and 4 large Stones weighing about One Hundred and Fifty or Two Hundred Pound each, was blown down from the end of the Church, three of the four Iron Spears, that stood with Vanes on the corners of the Tower, were broke short off in the middle, and the Vanes not to be found, and the Tail of the Weather Cock, which stood in the middle of the Tower was blown off, and found in a Court near 400 yards distant from the Tower. In Cline Wood belonging to the Duke of Beaufort[4] near this Townm, there is about 100 large Trees blown down; as also in a Wood on our River belonging to Mr. *Thomas Manfell* of *Brittonferry* about 80 large Oakes. The Tydes did not much damage, but two Ships were blown off our Bar, and by Providence one came aground on the Salt House point near our Harbour, else the Ship and Men had perished; the other came on shore, but was saved. I hear further, that there are several Stacks of Corn over-turn'd by the violence of the Wind, in the Parishes of *Roysily* and *Largenny* in *Gower*; most of the Thatcht Houses in this Neighbourhood was uncovered. Sir, this you may rely on to be true,

Yours, &c.
William Jones.

---

4   Henry Somerset, the 2nd Duke of Beaufort (1684 - 1714). —Ed.

From Grimsby *in* Lincolnshire, *the following Account is taken for favourable.*

S I R,

The late dreadful Tempest did not (Blessed be God) much affect us on shore, so far was it from having any events more than common, that the usual marks of ordinary Storms are not to be met with in these parts upon the Land. I wish I could give as good an Account of the Ships then at Anchor in our Road, the whole Fleet consisted of about an hundred Sail, fifty whereof were wanting after the Storm. The Wrecks of four are to be seen in the Road at low Water then Men all lost, three more were sunk near the Spurn, all the Men but one saved, six or seven were driven ashoar, and got off again with little or no damage. A small Hoy, not having a Man on Board, was taken at Sea, by a Merchant Ship, what became of the rest, we are yet to learn. This is all the Account I am able to give of the effects of the late Storm, which was so favourable to us. I am

Sir, Tour most Humble Servant,
Tho. Fairweather.

From Newport *and* Hastings *the following Accounts are chiefly mentioned to confirm what we have from other Inland parts, and particularly in the Letter Printed in the* Philosophical Transactions, *concerning the Salt being found on the Grass and Trees, at great distance from the Sea, of which there are very Authentick Relations.*

S I R,

I received yours, and do hereby give you the best account of what hapned by the late Storm in our Island; we have had several Trees blown down, and many Houses in our Town, and all parts of the Inland partly uncovered, but Blessed be God not one Person perisht that I know or have heard of; nor one Ship, or Vessel stranded on our shores in that dreadful Storm, but only one Vessel laden with Tin, which was driven from her Anchors in Cornwal, but was not stranded here till the *Tuesday* after, having spent her Main-mast and all her Sails. On Sunday night last we had several Ships and Vessels stranded on the South and South West parts of our Island; but reports are so various, that I cannot tell you how many, some fay 7, others 8, 12, and some fay 15; one or two laden with Cork, and two or three with Portugal Wine, Oranges and Lemons, one with Hides and Butter, one with Sugar, one with Pork, Beef and Oatmeal, and one with Slates. Monday night, Tuesday and

Wednesday came on the back of our Island,and some in at the Needles, the Fleet that went out with the King of Spain, but it has been here such a dreadful Storm, and such dark weather till this Afternoon, that we can give no true account of them; some fay that have been at the Wrecks this Afternoon, that there were several great Ships coming in then: There is one thing I had almost forgotten, and I think is very remarkable, that there was found on the Hedges and Twigs of Trees, knobs of Salt Congeal'd, which must come from the South and South Weft parts of our Sea Coast, and was seen and tasted at the distance of 6 and 10 miles from those Seas, and this account I had myself from the mouths of several Gentlemen of undeniable Reputation,

Yours,
Tho. Reade.

Hastings in Sussex, Jan. 25. 1703.

S I R,

ou desire to know what effect the late dreadful Storm of Wind had upon this Town; in answer to your desire, take the following Account. This Town consists of at least 600 Houses, besides two great Churches, some Publick Buildings, and many Shops standing upon the Beach near the Sea, and yet by the special Blessing and Providence of God, the whole Town suffered not above 30 or 40 *l.* damage in their Houses, Churches, Publick Building and Shops, and neither Man, Woman or Child suffered the least hurt by the said Terrible Storm. The Town stands upon the Sea shore, but God be thanked no damage; and the Tydes were not so great as we have seen upon far less Storms. The Wind was exceeding Boisterous, which might drive the Froth and Sea moisture six or seven miles up the Country, for at that distances from the Sea, the Leaves of the Trees and Bushes, were as Salt as if they had been dipped in the Sea, which can be imputed to nothing else, but the Violent Winds carrying the Frosth and Moisture so far. I believe it may be esteemed almost Miraculous that our Town escaped so well in the late terrible Storm, and therefore I have given you this Account. I am

Sir, your Friend,
Stephen Gawen

The following melancholy Account from the Town of Brighthemstone *in Sussex is sent us.*

S I R,

he late dreadful Tempest in Novemb. 27. 1703. last, had very terrible Effects in this Town. It began here much about One of the Clock in the Morning, the violence of the Wind stript a great many Houses, turn'd up the Leads off the Church, over-threw two Windmills, and laid them flat on the ground, the Town in general (upon the approach of Day-light) looking as if it had been Bombarded. Several Vessels belonging to this Town were loft, others stranded, and driven ashoar, others forced over to *Holland* and *Hamborough*, to the great Impoverishment of the Place. *Derick Pain,* Junior, Master of the *Elizabeth* Ketch of this Town lost, with all his Company. *George Taylor*, Master of the *Ketch* call'd the *Happy Entrance*, lost, and his Company, excepting *Walter Street*, who swiming three days on a Mast between the *Downs* and *North Yarmouth*, was at last taken up. *Richard Webb*, Master of the Ketch call'd the *Richard* and *Rose* of *Brighthelmston*, lost, and all his Company near St. *Hellens*. Edward Friend, Master of the *Ketch* call'd *Thomas and Francis*, stranded near *Portsmouth*: *Edward Glover*, Master of the Pink call'd *Richard and Benjamin*, stranded near *Chichester*, lost one of his Men, and he, and the rest of his Company, forced to hang in the Shrouds sever-

187

al hours. *George Beach*, Junior, Master of the Pink call'd *Mary*, driven over to *Hamborough* from the *Downes*, having lost his Anchor, Cables and Sails. Robert Kichener, Master of the *Cholmley* Pink of *Brighton*, lost near the *Roseant* with nine Men, five Men and a Boy saved by another Vessel. This is all out of this Town, besides the loss of several other able Seamen belonging to this Place, aboard of her Majesty's Ships, Transports and Tenders.

From Lymington and Lyme *we have the following Letters;*

S I R,

receiv'd I your Letter, and have made Enquiry concerning what Disasters happen'd during the late Storm; what I can learn at present, and that may be credited, are these, That a *Guernsey* Privateer lost his Fore-top mast, and cut his main Mast by the Board, had 12 Men wash'd over board, and by the toss of another immediate Sea three of them was put on board again, and did very well this was coming within the *Needles* That six Stacks of Chimnies were, by the violence of the Wind, blown from a great House call'd *New Park* in the *Forrest*, some that food directly to Windward, were blown clear off the House without injuring the Roof, or damaging the House, or any mischief to the Inhabitants, and fell some Yards from the House. Almost 4000 Trees were torn up by the roots within her Majesty's Forrest call'd *New Forrest*, some of them of very great bulk, others small, &c. A Ship of about 200 Tun, from *Maryland*, laden with Tobacco, call'd the *Assistance*, was Cast away upon Hurt Beach, one of the Mates, and 4 Sailors, were left. By the flowing of the Sea over Hurst Beach, two Saltterns were almost ruin'd belonging to one Mr. *Perkins*. A new Barn, nigh this Town, was blown quite down. The Town receiv'd not much damage, only some Houses being stript of the Healing, Windows broke, and a Chimney or two blown down. Considerable damages amongst the Farmers in the adjacent Places, by over-turning Barns, Outhouses, Stacks of Corn and Hay, and also amongst poor Families, and small Houses, and likewise abundance of Trees of all forts, especially Elms and Apple-Trees, has been destroy'd upon the several Gentlemen's, and others Estates hereabouts. These are the most remarkable Accidents that I can Collect at present; if any thing occur, it shall be sent you by

Your humble Servant,
James Baker.

Lymington, *Feb.* 1704.

A True and exact Account of the Damages done by the late great Wind in the Town of Lyme Regis, *and parts adjacent in the County of* Dorset, *as followeth,*

S I R

mpri. Five Boats drove out of the Cob and one Vessel lost, broke loose all but one Cabel, and swung out of the Cob, but was got in again with little Damage; and had that Hurricane happened here at High Water, the Cob must without doubt have been destroyed, and all the Vessels in it been lost, most of the Houses had some Damage: Buta great many Trees blown up by the Roots in our Neighbourhood, and four Miles to the Eastward of this Town: A *Guernsey* Privateer of eight Guns, and 43 Men drove Ashoar shoar, and but three Men saved of the 43; the place where the said Privateer run Ashoar, is call'd Sea Town, half a Mile from *Chidock*, where most of there Houses were uncovered, and one Man killed as he lay in Bed: This is the true Account here, but all Villages suffered extreamly in Houses, Trees, both Elem and Apples without Number.

Sir, I am your humble Servant,
Stephen Bowdidge.

From Margate, and the land of Thanet in Kent, the following is an honest Account.

S I R,

he following Account is what I can I give you, of what Damage is done in this Inland in the late great Storm; in this Town hardly a House escaped without Damage, and for the most part of them the Tiles blown totally off from the Roof, and several Chimneys blown down, that broke through part of the Houses to the Ground, and several Families very narrowly escaped being kill'd in their Beds, being by Providence just got up, so that they escaped, and none was kill'd; the like Damages being done in most little Towns and Villages upon this Island, as likewise Barns, Stables and Out- housing blown down to the Ground in a great many Farm - houses and Villages within the Island, part of the Leads of our Church blown clear off, and a great deal of Damage to the Church it self; likewise a great deal of Damage to the Churches of St. Lawrance Minter, Mounton and St. Nichola: In this Road was blown out one Latchford of Sandwich bound home from London, with divers Men and Women passengers all totally loft: And another little Pink that is not heard of blown away at the fame time, but where it belonged is not known; here rid out the Storm the Princess Anne, Captain Charles Gye, and the Swan, both Hospital Ships, had no Damage, only Captain Gye was parted from one of his Anchors, and part of à Cable which was weigh'd and carry'd after him to the River, by one of our Hookers. All from

Yours to Command,
P. H.

From Malden *in* Essex, *and from* Southampton, *the following Accounts,*

S I R,

By the late great Storm our Damages were considerable. A Spire of a Steeple blown down: Several Vessels in this Harbour were much shatter'd, particularly one Corn Vessel laden for *London*, stranded, and the Corn lost to the Value of about 500 *l.* and the Persons narrowly escaped by a small Boat that relieved them next Day: Many Houses ript up, and some blown down: The Churches shatter'd, and the principal Inn of this Town thirty or forty pound Damage in Tilling: At a Gentleman's House (one Mr. *Moses Bourton*) near us, a Stack of Chimneys blown down, fell through the Roof upon a Bed, where his Children was, who were drag'd out, and they narrowly escaped; many other Chimney's blown down here, and much Mischief done.

Southampton, February the 7th 170¼.

S I R,

Yours I have receiv'd, in which you desire me to give you an Account of what remarkable Damage the late violent Storm hath done at this place; in answer, We had most of the Ships in our River, and those that laid off from our Keys blown Ashoar, some partly torn to Wrecks, and three or four blown so far on Shoar with the Violence of the Wind, that the Owners have been at the Charges of unlading them, and dig large Channels for the Spring Tides to float them off, and with much a do have got them off, it being on a soft Sand or Mud, had but little Damage; we had, God be prais'd no body drowned, tho' some narrowly Escape't: As to our Town it being most part old Building, we have suffer'd much, few or no Houses have escape't: Several Stacks of Chimneys blown down, other Houses most part untiled: Several People bruis'd, but none kill'd: Abundance of Trees round about us, especially in the New Forest blown down; others with their Limbs of a great bigness torn; it being what we had most Material. I rest,

Sir, your humble Servant,
Geo. Powell.

We have abundance of strange Accounts from other Parts, and particularly the following Letter from the Downs, and tho' every Circumstance in this Letter is not litterally True, as to the Number of Ships, or Lives lost, and the stile Course, and Sailor like; yet I have inserted this Letter, because it seems to describe the Horror and Consternation the poor Sailors were in at that time. And because this is Written from one, who was as near an Eye Witness as any could possible be, and be safe.

S I R,

These Lines I hope in God will find you in good Health, we are all left here in a dismal Condition, expecting every moment to be all drowned For here is a great Storm, and is very likely to continue; we have here the Rear Admiral of the Blew in the Ship, call'd the Mary, a third Rate, the very next Ship to ours, sunk, with Admiral Beaumont, and above 500 Men drowned: The-Ship call'd the *Northumberland*, a third Rate, about 500 Men all sunk and drowned: The Ship call'd the *Sterling Castle*, a third Rate, all sunk and drowned above 500 Souls: And the Ship call'd the *Restoration*, a third Rate, all sunk and drowned: These Ships were all close by us which I saw; these Ships fired their Guns all Night and Day long, poor Souls, for help, but the Storm being so fierce and raging, could have none to save them: The Ship call'd the *Shrewsberry* that we are in, broke two Anchors, and did run mighty fierce backwards, within 60 or 80 Yards of the Sands, and as God Almighty would have it, we flung our sheet Anchor down, which is the biggest, and so stopt: Here we all pray'd to God to forgive us our Sins, and to save us, or else to receive us into his Heavenly Kingdom. If our sheer Anchor had given way, we had been all drown'd: But I humbly thank God, it was his gracious Mercy that saved us. There's one Captain Fanel's Ship, three Hospital Ships, all split, some sunk, and most of the Men drown'd.

There are above 40 Merchant Ships cast away and sunk: To see. Admiral Beaumont, that was next us, and all the rest of his Men, how they climed up the main Mast, hundreds at a time crying out for help, and thinking to save their Lives, and in the twinkling of an Eye were drown'd: I can give you no Account, but of these four Men of War aforesaid, which I saw with my own Eyes, and those Hospital Ships, at present, by reason the Storm hath drove us far distant from one another: Captain Crow, of our Ship, believes we have lost several more Ships of War, by reason we see so few; we lye here in great danger, and waiting for a North Easterly Wind to bring us to *Portsmouth,* and it is our Prayers to God for it; for we know not how soon this Storm may arise, and cut us all off, for it is a dismal Place to Anchor in. I have not had my Cloaths off, nor a wink of

Sleep these four Nights, and have got my Death with cold almost.

Yours to Command,
Miles Norcliffe

I send this, having opportunity by our Botes, that went Ashoar to carry some poor Men off, that were almost dead, and were taken up Swimming.

The following Letter is yet more Particular and Authentick, and being better exprest, may further describe the Terror of the Night in this place.

S I R,

I understand you are a Person concerned in making up a Collection of some remarkable accidents that happened by the Violence of the late dreadful Storm. I here present you with one of the like. I presume you never heard before, nor hope may never hear again of a Ship that was blown from her Anchors out of *Helford Haven* to the Isle of Wight, in less than eight hours, viz. The Ship lay in *Helford Haven* about two Leagues and a half Westward of *Falmouth*, being laden with Tin, which was taken on Board from *Guague* Wharf, about five or fix miles up *Helford* River, the Commanders name was *Anthony Jenkins*, who lives at *Falmouth*. About eight a Clock in the Evening before the Storm begun, the said Commander and Mate came on Board, and ordered the Crew that he left on Board, which was but one Man and 2 Boys; that if the Wind should chance to blow hard (which he had some apprehension of) to carry out the small Bower Anchor, and moor the Ship by 2 Anchors, and gave them some other orders, and his Mate and he went ashoar, and left the Crew aforesaid on Board; about nine a Clock the Wind began to blow, then they carried out the small Bower (as directed; it continued blowing harder and harder at West North West, at last the Ship began to drive, then they were forced to let go the best Bower Anchor which brought the Ship up. The Storm increasing more, they let go the Kedge Anchor, which was all they had to let go, so that the Ship rid with four Anchors a head: Between eleven and twelve a Clock the Wind came about West and by South in a most Terrible and Violent manner, that notwithstanding a very high Hill just to Windward of the Ship, and four Anchors ahead,, she was drove from all her Anchors; and about twelve a Clock drove out of the Harbour, without Anchor or Cable, nor so much as a Boat left in case they could put into any Harbour. In dreadful condition the Ship drove out clear of the Rocks to Sea, where the Man with the two Boys consulted what to do, at last resolve d to keep her far enough to Sea, for fear of *Deadman's Head*, being a point of Land between *Falmouth* and *Plim-*

outh, the latter of which places they designed to run her in, if possible, to save their Lives; the next morning in this frighted condition they steer'd her clear of the Land (to the best of their skill) sometimes almost under Water, and sometimes a top, with only the bonet of her Foresail out, and the Fore yard almost lower'd to the Deck; but instead of getting into *Plymouth* next day as intended, they were far enough, off that Port, for the next morning they saw Land, which proved to be Peverel Point, a little to the Westward of the *Isle of Wight*; so that they were in a worse Consternation then before, for over-running their designed Port by seven a Clock, they found themselves off the *Isle of Wight*; where they confuted again what to do to save their Lives, one of the Boys was for running her into the *Downs*, but that was objected against, by reason they had no Anchors nor Boat, and the Storm blowing off shore in the Downs, they should be blown on the unfortunate Goodwin Sands and lost. Now comes the last cousultation for their lives, there was one of the Boys said he had been in a certain Creek in the *Isle of Wight*, were between the Rocks he believed there was room enough to run the Ship in and save their Lives; and desired to have the Helm from the Man, and he would venture to steer the Ship into the said place, which he according did, where there was only just room between Rock and Rock for the Ship to come in, where she gave one blow or two against the Rocks, and funk immediately, but the Man and two Boys jumpt ashore, and all the Lading being Tin was saved, (and for their Conduct and Risk they run) they were all very well gratified, and the Merchants well satisfied.

Your Friend and Servant,
R. P.

May 28. 1704.

And here I cannot omit that great Notice has been taken of the Towns-people of *Deal* who are blam'd, and I doubt not with too much Reason for their great Barbarity in neglecting to save the Lives of abundance of poor Wretches; who having hung upon the Masts and Rigging of the Ships, or floated upon the broken Pieces of Wrecks, had gotten a Shore upon the *Goodwin Sands* when the Tide was out.

It was, without doubt, a sad Spectale to behold the poor Seamen walking to and fro upon the Sands, to view their Postures, and the Signals they made for help, which, by the Assistance of Glasses was easily seen from the Shore.

Here they had a few Hours Reprieve, but had neither present Refreshment, nor any hopes of Life, for they were sure to be all wash'd into another World at the Reflux of the Tide. Some Boats are said to come very near them in quest of Booty, and in search of Plunder, and to carry off what they could get, but no Body concern'd themselves for the Lives of these miserable Creatures.

And yet I cannot but incert what I have re-ceiv'd from very good Hands in behalf of one Person in that Town, whose Humanity deserves this remembrance, and I am glad of the Oppor-tunity of doing some Justice in this Case to a Man of so much Charity in a Town of so little.

Mr. *Thomas Powell*, of *Deal*, a Slop-Seller by Trade, and at that time Mayor of the Town. The Character of his Person I need not dwell upon here, other than the ensuing Accounts will de-scribe, for when I have said he is a Man of Char-ity and Courage, there is little I need to add to it, to move the Reader to value both his Person, and his Memory; and tho' I am otherwise a per-fect Stranger to him, I am very well pleased to transmit to Posterity the Account of his Behav-iour, as an Example to all good Christians to im-itate on the like Occasions.

He found himself mov'd with Compassion at the Distresses of the poor Creatures, whom he saw as aforesaid in that miserable Condition upon the Sands, and the first Thing he did, he made Application to the Custom-House Of-ficers for the Assistance of their Boats and Men, to save the Lives of as many as they could come at, the Custom House Men rudely refus'd, either to send their Men, or to part with their Boats.

Provoked with the unnatural Carriage of the Custom House Officers, he calls the People about him; and finding some of the Common People began to be more than ordinarily af-fected with the Distresses of their Countrymen, and as he thought a little enclin'd to venture; he made a general Offer to all that would ven-ture out, that he would pay them out of his own Pocket. 5 s. *per head* for all the Men whose

Lives they could save, upon this Proposal several offered themselves to go, if he would furnish 'em with Boats.

Finding the main Point clear, and that he had brought the Men to be willing, he with their Assistance took away the Custom House Boats by Force; and tho' he knew he could not justify it, and might be brought into Trouble for it, and particularly if it were lost, might be oblig'd to pay for it, yet he resolv'd to venture that, rather than hazard the loss of his Design, for the saving so many poor Men's Lives, and having Mann'd their Boat with a Crew of four honest Fellows, he with them took away several other Boats from other Persons, who made use of them only to Plunder and Rob, not regarding the Distresses of the poor Men.

Being thus provided both with Men and Boats he sent them off, and by this means brought on Shore above 200 Men, whose Lives a few Minutes after, must infallibly ha' been lost.

Nor was this the End of his Care, for when the Tide came in, and 'twas too late to go off again, for that all that were left were swallow'd up with the Raging of the Sea, his Care was then to relieve the poor Creatures, who he had sav'd, and who almost dead with Hunger and Cold, were naked and starving.

And first he applied himself to the Queen's Agent *for Sick and Wounded Seamen,* but he would not relieve them with One Penny, whereupon, at his own Charge, he furnish'd them with Meat, Drink and Lodging.

The next Day several of them died, the Extremities they had suffer'd, having too much Master'd their Spirits, these he was forc'd to

bury also at his own Charge, the Agent still re-
fusing to Disburse one Penny. After their Refreshment the poor Men assisted by the May-
or, made a fresh Application to the Agent for
Conduct Money to help them up to *London*,
but he answer'd he had no Order, and would
Disburse nothing whereupon the Mayor gave
them all Money in their Pockets, and Passes to
Graves-End.

I wish I could say with the same Freedom,
that he receiv'd the Thanks of the Government,
and Reimbursement of his Money as he de-
serv'd, but in this I have been inform'd, he met
with great Obstructions and Delays, tho' at last,
after long Attendance, upon a right Application
I am inform'd he obtain'd the repayment of his
Money, and some small Allowance for his Time
spent in solliciting for it.

Nor can the Damage suffered in the River of
Thames be forgot. It was a strange sight to see
all the Ships in the River blown away, the Pool
was so clear, that, as I remember, not above 4
Ships were left between the Upper part of Wap-
ping, and Ratcliff Cross, for the Tide being up at
the Time when the Storm blew with the greatest
violence. No Anchors or Landfast, no Cables or
Moorings would hold them, the Chains which
lay cross the River for the mooring of Ships, all
gave way.

The Ships breaking loose thus, it must be a
strange sight to see the Hurry and Confusion
of it, and as some Ships had no Body at all on
Board, and a great many had none but a Man or
Boy left on Board just to look after the Vessel,
there was nothing to be done, but to let every
Vessel drive whither and how she would.

Those who know the Reaches of the River, and how they lye, know well enough, that the Wind being at South West Westerly, the Vessels would naturally drive into the Bite or Bay from Ratcliff Cross to Lime- house Hole, for that the River winding about again from thence towards the New Dock at Deptford, runs almost due South West, so that the Wind blew down one Reach, and up another, and the Ships must of necessity drive into the bottom of the Angle between both.

This was the Cafe, and as the Place is not large, and the Number of Ships very great, the force of the Wind had driven them so into one another, and laid them so upon one another as it were in heaps, that I think Man may safely defy all the World to do the like.

The Author of this Collection had the curiosity the next day to view the place, and to observe the posture they lay in, which nevertheless 'tis impossible to describe; there lay, by the best Account he could take, few less than 700 fail of Ships, some very great ones between *Shadwel* and *Limehouse* inclusive, the posture is not to be imagined, but by them that saw it, some Vessels lay heeling off with the Bow of another Ship over her Waste, and the Stem of another upon her Fore-Castle, the Boltsprits of some drove into the Cabbin Windows of others; some lay with their Sterns tossed up so high, that the Tide flowed into their Fore-Castles before they cou'd come to Rights; some lay so leaning upon others, that the undermost Vessels wou'd sink before the other could float; the numbers of Masts, Boltsprits and Yards split and broke, the staving the Heads, and Sterns and Carved Work, the tearing and destruction of Rigging, and the squeezing of Boats to pieces between the Ships, is not to be reckened; but there was hardly a Vessel to be seen that had not suffer'd some damage or other in one or all of these Articles.

There was several Vessels sunk in this hurry, but as they were generally light Ships, the damage was chiefly to the Vessels; but there were two Ships sunk with great quantity of Goods on Board, the Russel Galley was sunk at *Limehouse*, being a great part laden with Bale Goods for the *Streights*, and the *Sarah* Gally lading for *Leghorn*, sunk at an Anchor at *Blackwall*; and though she was afterwards weighed and brought on shore, yet her back was broke, or so otherwise disabled, as she was never fit for the Sea; there were several Men drown'd in these last two Vessels, but we could never come to have the particular number.

Near *Gravesend* several Ships drove on shoar below *Tilbury* Fort, and among them five bound for the *West Indies*, but as the shoar is ouzy and soft, the Vessels sat upright and easy, and here the high Tides which follow'd, and which were the ruin of so many in other places, were the deliverance of all these Ships whose lading and value was very great, for the Tide rising to an unusual height, floated them all off, and the damage was not so great as was expected.

If it be expected I should give an account of the loss, and the particulars relating to small Craft, *as the Sailors call it*, in the River it is to look for what is impossible, other than by generals.

The Watermen tell us of above 500 Wherries lost, most of which were not sunk only but dasht to pieces one against another, or against the

Shores and Ships, where they lay: Ship Boats without number were driven about in every corner, sunk and staved, and about 300 of them is supposed to be lost. Above 60 Barges and Lighters were found driven foul of the *Bridge*; some Printed accounts tell us of sixty more sunk or staved between the *Bridge* and *Hammersmith.*

Abundance of Lighters and Barges drove quite thro' the *Bridge*, and took their fate below, whereof many were lost, so that we Reckon by a modest account above 100 Lighters and Barges lost and spoil'd in the whole, not reckoning such as with small damage were recovered.

In all this confusion it could not be, but that many Lives were loft, but as the *Thames* often times Buries those it drowns, there has been no account taken. Two Watermen at *Black Fryars* were drowned, endeavouring to save their Boat; and a Boar was said to be Overset near *Fulham*, and five People drown'd: According to the best account I have seen, about 22 People were drown'd in the River upon this sad occasion, which considering all circumstances is not a great many, and the damage to Shipping computed with the vast number of Ships then in the River, the Violence of the Storm, and the heighth of the Tide, confirms me in the Truth of that Opinion, which I have heard many skilful Men own, *viz.* that the River of *Thames* is the best Harbour of Europe.

The highth of the Tide, as I have already observ'd, did no great damage in the River of *Thames*, and I find none of the Levels or Marshes, which lye on both sides the River overflowed with it, it fill'd the Cellars indeed at *Gravesend*, and on both sides in *London*, and the Ale-house-keepers suffered some loss as to their Beer, but this damage is not worth mentioning with what our Accounts give us from the Severn; which, besides the particular Letters we have already quoted, the Reader may observe in the following. what our general intelligence furnishes us with.

The Damages in the City of *Gloucester* they compute at 12000 *l.* above 15000 Sheep drown'd in the Levels on the side of the *Severne*, and the Sea Walls will cost, as these Accounts tell us, 5000. to repair, all the Country lyes under Water for 20 or 30 Miles together on both sides, and the Tide rose three Foot higher than the tops of the Banks.

At *Bristol* they tell us, The Tide fill'd their Cellars, spoil'd 1000 Hogsheads of Stigar, 1500 Hogsheads of Tobacco, and the Damage they reckon at 100000 *l.* Above 80 People drown'd in the Marshes and River, several whole Families perishing together. The Harbour at *Plimouth*, the Castle at *Pendennis*, the Cathederal at *Gloucester*, the great Church at *Berkely*, the Church of St. *Stephen*'s at Bristol; the Churches at *Blandford*, at *Bridgewater*, at *Cambridge*, and generally the Churches all over *England* have had a great share of the Damage.

In *King Road* at *Bristol*, the Damage by Sea is also very great; the *Canterbury* store Ship was driven on Shoar, and twenty-five of her Men drown'd, as by our account of the Navy will more particularly appear, the *Richard* and *John*, the *George*, and the *Grace* sunk, and the number of People loft is variously reported.

These Accounts in the four last Paragraphs being abstracted from the publick Prints, and what other Persons collect, I desire the Reader will observe, are not particularly vouch'd, but as they are all true in substance, they are so far to be depended upon, and if there is any mistake it relates to Numbers, and quantity only. From *Yarmouth* we expected terrible News, and every one was impatient till they saw the Accounts from thence, for as there was a very great Fleet there, both of laden Colliers, Russia Men, and others, there was nothing to be expected but a dreadful Destruction among them.

But it pleas'd God to order Things there, that the loss was not in Proportion like what it was in other Places, not but that it was very great too.

The *Reserve* Man of War was come in but a day or two before, Convoy to the great Fleet from *Russia*, and the Captain, Surgeon and Clerk, who after so long a Voyage went on Shoar with two Boats to refresh themselves, and buy Provisions, had the Mortification to stand on Shoar, and fee the Ship sink before their Faces; she foundred about 11-a-Clock, and as the Sea went too high for any help to go off from the Shoar to them, so their own Boats being both on Shoar, there was not one Man sav'd; one *Russia* Ship driving from her Anchors, and running foul of a laden Collier sunk by his side, but some of her Men were sav'd by getting on Board the Collier; three or four small Vessels were driven out to Sea, and never heard of more; as for the Colliers, tho' most of them were driven from their Anchors yet going away to Sea, we have not an account of many lost.

This next to the Providence of God, I give this reason for, first by all Relations it appears that the Storm was not so violent farther Northward, as it was there; and as it was not so Violent, so neither did it continue so long: Now those Ships, who found they could not ride it out in *Yarmouth* Roads, but flipping their Cables went away to Sea, possibly as they went away to the Northward, found the Weather more moderate at least, not so violent, but it might be borne with, to this may be added, that 'tis well known to such as use the Coast after they had run the length of *Flambro*, they had the benefit of the Weather Shoar, and pretty high land, which if they took shelter under might help them very much; these, with other Circumstances, made the Damage much less than every Body expected, and yet as it was, it was bad enough as our Letter from *Hull* gives an Account. At *Grimsby* it was still worse as to the Ships, where almost all the Vessels were blown out of the Road, and a great many lost.

At *Plymouth* they felt a full Proportion of the Storm in its utmost fury, the Edystone has been mention'd already, but it was a double loss in that, the light House had not been long down, when the *Winchelsea*, a homeward bound *Virginia* Man was split upon the Rock, where that Building flood, and most of her Men drowned.

Three other Merchant Ships were cast away in *Plimouth* Road, and most of their Men lost: The *Monk* Man of War rod it out, but was oblig'd to cut all her Masts by the Board, as several Men of War did in other places.

At *Portsmouth* was a great Fleet, as has been noted already, several of the Ships were blown quite out to Sea, whereof some were never heard of more; the *Newcastle* was heard off upon the Coast of *Sussex*, where she was lost with all their Men but 23; the *Resolution*, the Eagle advice Boat, and the *Litchfield Prize* felt the same fate, only sav'd their Men: From Cows several Ships were driven out to Sea, whereof one run on Shoar in Stokes -bay, one full of Soldiers, and two Merchant Men have never been heard off, as I could ever learn, abundance of the Ships sav'd themselves by cutting down their Masts, and others Stranded, but by the help of the ensuing Tides got off again.

Portsmouth, *Plymouth*, *Weymouth*, and most of our Sea Port Towns look'd as if they had been Bombarded, and the Damage of them is not easily computed.

Several Ships from the *Downs* were driven over to the Coast of *Holland*, and some sav'd themselves there; but several others were lost there.

At *Falmouth* 11 Sail of Ships were stranded on the Shoar, but most of them got off again.

In *Barstable* Harbour, a Merchant Ship outward bound was over-set, and the express advice Boat very much shatter'd, and the Key of the Town almost destroy'd.

'Tis endless to attempt any farther Description of Losses, no place was free either by Land or by Sea, every thing that was capable felt the fury of the Storm; and 'tis hard to say, whether was greater the loss by Sea, or by Land; the Multitude of brave stout Sailors is a melancholy subject, and if there be any difference gives the fad Balance to the Account of the Damage by Sea.

We had an Account of about 11 or 12 Ships droven over for the Coast of *Holland*, most of which were lost, but the Men saved, so that by the best Calculation I can make, we have not lost less than 150 sail of Vessels of all sorts by the Storm; the number of Men and other damages, are Calculated elsewhere.

We have several Branches of this Story which at first were too easily credited, and put in Print, but upon more strict examination, and by the discoveries of Time, appear'd otherwise, and therefore are not set down.

It was in the design to have Collected the several Accounts of the fatal effects of the Tempest abroad in Foreign Parts; but as our Accounts came in from thence too imperfect to be depended upon; the Collector of these Papers could not be satisfied to offer them to the World, being willing to keep as much as possible to the Terms of his Preface.

We are told there is an Abstract to the same purpose with this in *France*, Printed at *Paris*, and which contains a strange variety of Accidents in that Country.

If a particular of this can be obtained, the Author Promises to put it into *English*, and adding to them the other Accounts, which the rest of the World can afford, together with some other Additions of the *English* Affairs, which could not be obtain'd in time here shall make up the second part of this Work.

In the mean time the Reader may observe, *France* felt the general shock the Peers, and Ricebank at *Dunkirk*, the Harbour at *Haver de Grace*, the Towns of Calais and Bulloign give us strange Accounts.

All the Vessels in the Road before *Dunkirk*, being 23 or 17, I am not certain, were dasht in pieces against the Peer Heads, not one excepted, that side being a Lee shoar, the reason is plain, there was no going off to Sea; and had it been so with us in the *Downs* or *Yarmouth* Roads, it would have fared with us in the same manner, for had there been no going off to Sea, 300 fail in *Yarmouth* Roads had inevitably perisht.

At *Diepe* the like mischief happened, and in proportion *Paris* felt the effects of it, as bad as *London*, and as a Gentleman who came from thence since that time, affirmed it to me it was much worse.

All the N. East Countries felt it, in *Holland* our accounts in general are very dismal, but the Wind not being N. W. as at former Storms, the Tyde did not drown them, nor beat so directly upon their Sea Wall.

It is not very irrational to Judge, that had the Storm beat more to the North West, it must have driven the Sea upon them in such a manner, that all their Dikes and Dams could not have sustained it, and what the consequence of such an Inundation might have been they can best judge, who remember the last terrible Irruption of the Sea there, which drowned several thousand People, and Cattle without number.

But as our Foreign Accounts were not satisfactory enough to put into this Collection, where we have promised to limit our selves by just Vouchers, we purposely refer it all to a farther description as before.

Several of our Ships were driven over to those parts, and some loft there, and the I story of our great Ships which rid it out, at or near the *Gunfleet*, should have come in here, if the Collector could have met with any Person that was in any of the said Vessels, but as the accounts he expected did not come in the time for the Impression, they were of necessity left out.

The *Association*, a Second Rate, on Board hereof was Sir *Stafford Fairborn*, was one of these, and was blown from the Mouth of the *Thames* to the Coast of *Norway*, a particular whereof as Printed in the Annals of the Reign of Queen Ann's is as follows.

An Account of Sir Stafford Fairborne's Distress in the late Storm.

S I R,

Her Majesty's Ship Association, a second Rate of 96 Guns, commanded by Sir *Stafford Fairborne*, Vice-Admiral of the Red, and under him Captain *Richard Canning*, failed from the *Downs* the 24th of *November* last, in Company with seven other Capital Ships, under the Command of the Honourable

Sir Cloudesley Shovel, Admiral of the White, in their return from Leghorn up the River. They anchored that Night off of the *Long-sand-head*. The next Day struck Yards and Top-Masts. The 27th about three in the Morning, the Wind at West South West, encreased to a Hurricane, which drove the *Association* from her Anchors. The Night was exceeding dark, but what was more Dreadful, the Galloper, a very dangerous Sand, was under her Lee; so that she was in Danger of striking upon it, beyond the Power of Man to avoid it. Driving thus at the Mercy of the Waves, it pleased God, that about five a Clock she passed over the tail of the Galloper in seven Fathom of Water. The Sea boisterous and angry, all in a Foam, was ready to swallow her up; and the Ship received at that time a Sea on her Starboard-side, which beat over all, broke and washed several half Ports, and forced in the entering Port. She took in such a vast quantity of Water, that it kept her down upon her side, and every Body believ'd, that he could not have risen again, had not the Water been speedily let down into the hold by scuttling the Decks. During this Consternation two of the Lower-Gun-Deck-Ports were pressed open by this mighty weight of Water, the most hazardous Accident, next to touching the Ground, that could have happened to us. But the Port, that had been forced open, being readily secured by the Direction and Command of the Vice- Admiral, who, though much indisposed, was upon, Deck all that time, prevented any farther Mischief. As the Ship still drove with the Wind, she was not long in this Shoal, (where it was impossible for any Ship to have lived at that time) but came into deeper Water, and then she had a smoother Sea. However the Hurricane did not abate, but rather seemed to gather Strength. For Words were no sooner uttered, but they were carried away by the Wind, so that although those upon Deck spoke loud and close to one another, yet they could not often distinguish what was said; and when they opened their Mouths, their Breath was almost taken away. Part of the Sprit Sail, tho' fast furled, was blown away from the Yard. A Ten-Oar- Boat, that was lashed on her Starboard-side, was often hove up by the Strength of the Wind, and over-set upon her Gun-Wale. We plainly saw the Wind skimming up the Water, as if it had been Sand, carrying it up into the Air, which was then so thick and gloomy, that Day light, which should have been comfortable to us, did, but make it appear more ghastly. The Sun by intervals peeped through the corner of a Cloud, but soon disappearing, gave us a more melancholick Prospect of the Weather. About in a Clock it dispersed the Clouds, and the Hurricane abated into a more moderate Storm, which drove us over to the Bank of *Flanders*, and thence along the Coast of *Holland* and *Friesland* to the entrance of the *Elb*, where the 4th of *December* we had almost as violent a Storm, as when we drove from our Anchors, the Wind at North West, driving us directly upon the Shoar. So that we must all have inevitably perished, had not God mercifully favoured us about 10 a Clock at night with a South West Wind, which gave us an opportunity to put to Sea. But being afterwards driven near the Coast of *Norway*, the Ship wanting Anchors and Cables, our Wood and Candles wholly expended; no Beer on Board, nor any thing else in lieu; every one reduced to one quart of Water *per* Day, the Men, who had been harassed at *Belle Isle*, and in our *Mediterrane-*

an Voyage, now jaded by the continual Fatigues of the Storms, falling sick every Day, the Vice-Admiral in this exigency thought it advisable to put into *Gottenbourgh*, the only Port where we could hope to be supplied. We arrived there the 11th of December, and having without lost of time got Anchors and Cables from *Copenhagen*, and Provisions from *Gottenbourgh*, we failed thence the Third of *January*, with twelve Merchant Men under our Convoy, all loaden with Stores for her Majesty's Navy. The Eleventh following we prevented four French Privateers from taking four of our Store- Ships. At Night we anchored off the *Long-Sand-Head*. Weighed again the next Day, but soon came to an Anchor, because it was very hazy Weather. Here we rid against a violent Storm, which was like to have put us to Sea. But after three Days very bad Weather, we weighed and arrived to the *Buoy of the Nore* the 23d of *January*, having run very great Risks among the Sands. For we had not only contrary Winds, but also very tempestuous Winds. We lost 28 Men by Sickness, contracted by the Hardships which they endur'd in the bad Weather; and had not Sir *Stafford Fairborne* by his great care and diligence, got the Ship out of *Gottenbourgh*, and by that prevented her being frozen up, most part of the Sailers had perished afterwards by the severity of the Winrer, which is intolerable Cold in those parts.

Of the Damage to the Navy

This is a short but terrible Article, there was
one Ship called the *Tork*, which was lost about
3 days before the great Storm off of *Harwich*,
but most of the Men were saved,

The loss immediately sustain'd in the Royal
Navy during the Storm, is included in the List
hereunto annex'd, as appears from the Navy
Books,

The damage done to the Ships that were sav'd,
is past our Power to compute. The Admiral, Sir
Cloudesley. Shovel with the great Ships, had
made sail but the day before out of the Downs,
and were taken with the Storm as they lay at or
near the Gunfleet, where they being well provided with Anchors and Cables, rid it out, tho' in
great extremity, expecting death every minute.

The loss of small Vessels hir'd into the Service, and tending the Fleet, is not included in
this, nor can well be, several such Vessels, and
some with Soldiers on Board, being driven away
to Sea, and never heard of more.

The loss of the Light-House, call'd the *Eddys-
tone* at *Plymouth*, is another Article, of which
we never heard any particulars other than this;
that at Night it was standing, and in the Morning all the upper part from the Gallery was
blown down, and all the People in it perished,
and by a particular Misfortune, Mr. Winstan-
ly, the Contriver of it, a Person whose loss is
very much regreted by such as knew him, as a
very useful Man to his Country: The loss of that
Light-House is also a considerable Damage,
as 'tis very doubtful whether it will be ever attempted again, and as it was a great Security to

the Sailors, many a good Ship having been loft there in former Times.

It was very remarkable, that, as we are inform'd, at the fame time the Light-House abovesaid was blown down, the Model of it in Mr. Windstanly's House at Littlebury in Essex, above 200 Miles from the Light-House, fell down, and was broken to pieces.

There are infinite Stories of like nature with these, the Disasters at Sea are full of a vast variety, what we have recommended to the view of the World in this History, may stand as an Abridgment; and the Reader is only to observe that these are the short Representations, by which he may guess at the most dreadful Night, these parts of the World ever saw.

To relate all Things, that report Furnishes us with, would be to make the story exceed common probability, and look like Romance.

'Tis a sad and serious Truth, and this part of it is preserv'd to Posterity to assist them in reflecting on the Judgments of God, and handing them on for the Ages to come.

Of the Earthquake

ho' this was some time after the Storm, yet as the Accounts of the Storm bring it with them in the following Letters, we cannot omit it.

The two following Letters are from the respective Ministers of Boston and Hull, and relate to the

Account of the Earthquake, which was felt over most part of the County of *Lincoln* and the *East Riding of Yorkshire*.

The Letter from *Hull*, from the Reverend Mr. Banks, Minister of the Place, is very particular, and deserves intire Credit, both from the extraordinary Character of the worthy Gentleman who writes it, and from its exact Correspondence with other Accounts.

S I R,

I receiv'd yours, wherein you acquaint me with a Design that (I doubt not) will meet with that Applause and Acceptance from the World which it deserves; but am in no capacity to be any way serviceable to it my self, the late Hurricane having more frighted than hurt us in these Parts. I doubt not but your Intelligence in general from the Northern Parts of the Nation, supplies you with as little Matter as what you have from these hereabouts, it having been less violent and mischievous that way. Some Stacks of Chimneys were over-turn'd here, and from one of them a little Child of my own was (thanks be to God) almost miraculously preserv'd, with a Maid that lay in the Room with him. I hear of none else this way that was so much as in danger, the Storm beginning here later than I perceive it did in some other Places, its greatest Violence being betwixt 7 and 8 in the Morning, when most People were stir ring.

The Earthquake, which the Publick Accounts mention to have happen'd at *Hull* and *Lincoln* upon the 28th *ult.* was felt here by some People about 6 in the Evening, at the same time that People there, as well as at *Grantham* and other Places, perceived it. We have some flying Stories about it which look like fabulous, whose Credit therefore I wou'd not be answerable for; as, that upon *Lincoln-Heath* the Ground was seen to open, and Flashes of Fire to issue out of the Chasm.

I doubt this Account will hardly be thought worth the Charge of Passage: Had there been any thing else of note, you had been very readly serv'd by,

S I R, *Your Humble Servant,*
E.K.

Boston, Jan. 8.
1703.

S I R,

I am afraid that you will believe me very rude, that yours, which I receiv'd the 12th of April, has not sooner receiv'd such an Answer as you expect and desire, and truly I think deserve; for, a Design so generous, as to undertake to transmit to Posterity, A Memorial of the dreadful Effects of the late terrible Tempest (that when

God's Judgments are in the World, they may be made so publick, as to ingage the Inhabitants of the Earth to learn Righteousness) ought to receive all possible Encouragement.

But the true Reason why I writ no sooner, was, Because, by the most diligent Enquiries I cou'd make, I cou'd not learn what Harm that dreadful Tempest did in the *Humber*; neither indeed can I yet give you any exact Account of it: for, the great Mischief was done in the Night; which was so Pitch-dark, that of above 8 Ships that then rid in the *Humber*, about *Grimsby Road*, very few escap'd some Loss or other, and none of 'em were able to give a Relation of any body but themselves.

The best Account of the Effects of the Storm in the *Humber*, that I have yet met with, I received but Yesterday, from Mr. *Peter Walls*, who is Master of that Watch-Tower, call'd the Spurn-Light, at the *Humber* Mouth, and was present there on the Night of the 26th of *November*, the fatal Night of the Storm. He did verily believe that his Pharos (which is above 20 Yards high) wou'd have been blown down; and the Tempest made the Fire in it burn so vehemently, that it melted down the Iron-bars on which it laid, like Lead; so that they were forced, when the Fire was by this means almost extinguished, to put in new Bars, and kindle the Fire a-fresh, which they kept in till the Morning Light appear'd: And then *Peter Walls* observed about fix or seven and twenty Sail of Ships, all driving about the *Spurn-Head*, some having cut, others broke their Cables, but all disabled, and render'd helpless.

These were a part of the two Fleets that then lay in the *Humber*, being put in there by stress of Weather a day or two before, some from *Russia*, and the rest of 'em Colliers, to and from *Newcastle*. Of these, three were driven upon an Island call'd the *Den*, within the *Spurn* in the Mouth of the *Humber*. The first of these no sooner touch'd Ground, but the over- set, and turn'd up her Bottom; out of which, only one of six (the Number of that Ship's Company) was lost, being in the Shrowds: the other five were taken up by the second Ship, who had sav'd their Boat. In this Boat were saved all the Men of the three Ships aforementioned (except as before excepted) and came to Mr. *Walls*'s House, at the Spurn Head, who got them good Fires, and all Accommodations necessary for them in such a Distress. The second Ship having no body aboard, was driven to Sea, with the Violence of the Tempest, and never seen or heard of more. The third, which was then a-ground, was (as he supposes) broken up and driven; for nothing, but some Coals that were in her, was to be seen the next Morning.

Another Ship, the Day after, *viz.* the 27th of *November*, was riding in *Grimsby Road*, and the Ships Company (except two Boys) being gone a-shore, the Ship, with the two Lads in her, drive directly out of *Humber*, and was lost, tho' 'tis verily believ'd the two Boys were saved by one of the Russia Ships, or Convoys.

The same Day, in the Morning, one *John Baines*, a *Yarmouth* Master, was in his Ship, riding in *Grimsby Road*, and by the Violence of the Storm, some other Ships coming foul upon him, part of his Ship was broken down, and was driven towards Sea; whereupon he anchored under *Kilnsey-Land*, and with his Crew came safe a shore, in his Boat, but the Ship was never seen more.

The remainder of the six or seven and twenty Sail aforesaid, being (as was before observed) driven out of the *Humber*, very few, if any of 'em, were ever heard of; and 'tis rationally believ'd, that all, or the most of them, perished. And indeed, altho' the Storm was not so violent here as it was about *Portsmouth*, *Yarmouth* Roads, and the Southern Coast, yet the Crews of the three Ships above-mentioned declare, that they were never out in so dismal a Night as that was of the 26th of *November*, in which the considerable Fleet aforesaid rid in *Grimsby Road* in the *Humber*; for most of the 80 Sail broke from their Anchors, and run foul one upon another; but by reason of the Darkness of the Night, they cou'd see very little of the Mischief that was done.

This is the best Account I can give you at present of the Effects of the Tempest in the *Humber*; whereas had the Enquiry been made immediately after the Storm was over, a great many more of remarkable Particulars might have been discover'd.

As to the Earthquake here, tho' I perceiv'd it not my self (being then walking to visit a sick Parishoner) yet it was so sensibly felt by so many Hundreds, that I cannot in the least question the Truth and Certainty of it.

It happen'd here, and in these Parts, upon *Innocent's* Day, the 28th of *December*, being Tuesday, about Five of the Clock in the Evening, or thereabout. Soon after I gave as particular Account as I cou'd learn of it, to that ingenious Antiquary Mr. *Thorsby* of *Leeds* in *Yorkshire*, but had no time to keep a Copy of my Letter to him, nor have I leisure to transcribe a Copy of this to you, having so constant a Fatigue of Parochial business to attend; nor will my Memory serve me to recollect all the Circumstances of that Earthquake, as I sent them to Mr. *Thoresby*; and possibly he may have communicated that Letter to you, or will upon your least intimation, being a generous Person, who loves to communicate any thing that may be serviceable to the Publick.

However, lest I shou'd seem to decline the gratifying your Request, I will recollect, and here set down, such of the Circumstances of that Earthquake as do at present occur to my Memory.

It came with a Noise like that of a Coach in the Streets, and mightily shak'd both the Glass Windows, Pewter, China Pots and Dishes, and in some places threw them down off the Shelves on which they flood. It did very little Mischief in this Town, except the throwing down a Piece of one Chimney. Several Persons thought that a great Dog was got under the Chair they fat upon; and others fell from their Seats, for fear of falling. It frighted several Persons, and caus'd 'em for a while to break off their Reading, or Writing, or what they were doing.

They felt but one Shake here: but a Gentleman in Nottinghamshire told me, that being then lame upon his Bed, he felt three Shakes, like the three Rocks of a Cradle, to and again.

At *Laceby* in *Lincolnshire*, and in several other Parts of that County, as well as of the Counties of *York* and *Nottingham*, the Earthquake was felt very sensibly; and particularly at *Laceby* aforesaid. There happen'd this remarkable Story.

On Innocent's Day, in the Afternoon, several Morrice-Dancers came thither from *Grimsby*; and after they had Danc'd and play'd their Tricks, they went towards *Alesby*, a little Town not far off: and as they were going about Five a Clock, they felt two such terrible Shocks of the Earth, that they had much ado to hold their Feet, and thought the Ground was ready to open, and swallow 'em up. Whereupon thinking that God was angry at 'em for playing the Fool, they return'd immediately to *Laceby* in a great Fright, and the next Day- home, not daring to pursue their intended Circuit and Dancing.

I think 'tis the Observation of Dr. *Willis*, that upon an Earthquake the Earth sends forth noisome Vapours which infect the Air, as the Air does our Bodies: and accordingly it has prov'd here, where we have ever since had a most sickly time, and the greatest Mortality that has been in this Place for 15 Years last past: and so I believe it has been over the greatest part of England. This, SIR, is the best Account I can give you of the Earthquake, which had com'd sooner, but that I was desirous to get likewise the belt Account I cou'd of the Effects of the Storm in the Humber. My humble Service to the Undertakers: and if in any thing I am capable to serve them or you, please freely to command,

S I R, *Your most humble Servant,*
Ro. Banks.

We have a farther Account of this in two Letters from Mr. *Thoresby,* F. R. S. and written to the Publisher of the *Philosophical Transactions,* and printed in their Monthly Collection, No. 289. as follows, which is the same mentioned by Mr. *Banks.*

Part of two Letters from Mr. Thoresby, *F. R. S. to the Publisher, concerning an Earthquake, which happen'd in some Places of the North of England, the 28th of* December 1703.

You have heard, no doubt, of the late *Earthquake* that affected some part of the North, as the dreadful Storm did the South. It being most observable at *Hull,* I was desirous of an Account from thence that might be depended upon; and therefore writ to the very obliging Mr. *Banks*, Prebendary of *York*, who being Vicar of *Hull*, was the most suitable Person I knew to address my self unto: and he being pleased to favour me with a judicious Account of it, I will venture to communicate it to you, with his pious Reflection thereupon.

As to the Earthquake you mention, it was felt here on *Tuesday* the 28th of the last Month, which was *Childermas Day*, about three or four Minutes after Five in the Evening. I confess I did not feel it my self; for I was at that moment walking to visit a sick Gentleman, and the Noise in the Streets, and my quick Motion, made it impossible, I believe, for me to feel it but it was so almost universally felt, that there can be no manner of doubt of the Truth of it.

Mr. *Peers*, my Reader, (who is an ingenious good Man) was then at his Study, and Writing; but the heaving up of his Chair and his Desk, the Shake of his Chamber, and the rattling of his Windows, did so amaze him, that he was really affrighted, and was forc'd for a while to give over his Work: and there are twenty such Instances amongst Tradesmen, too tedious to repeat. My Wife was then in her Closet, and thought her China would have come about her Ears, and my Family felt the Chairs mov'd, in which they were sitting by the Kitchen Fire-side, and heard such a Rattle of the Pewter and Windows as almost affrighted them. A Gentlewoman not far off said, her Chair lifted so high, that she thought the great Dog had got under it, and to save her self from falling, slipt off her Chair. I sent to a House where

part of a Chimney was shak'd down, to enquire
of the particulars; they kept Ale, and being pretty
full of Company that they were merry, they did
not perceive the Shock, only heard the Pewter
and Glass-windows dance; but the Landlady's
Mother, who was in a Chamber by her self, felt
the Shock so violent, that the verily believed the
House to be coming down (as part of the Chimney afore mention'd did at the same Moment)
and cried out in a Fright, and had fall'n, but that
the catched hold of a Table. It came and went
suddenly, and was attended with a Noise like the
Wind, though there was then a perfect Calm.

From other Hands I have an Account that it
was felt in *Beverly*, and other Places; at *South
Dalton* particularly, where the Parson's Wife (my
own Sifter) being alone in her Chamber, was sadly
frighted with the heaving up of the Chair she sat
in, and the very sensible Shake of the Room, especially the Widows, &c. A Relation of mine, who is a
Minister near *Lincoln*, being then at a Gentleman's
House in the Neighbourhood, was amaz'd at the
Moving of the Chairs they sat upon, which was so
violent, he writes every Limb of him was shaken; I
am told also from a true Hand, that so nigh us as
Selby, where Mr. Travers, a Minister, being in his
Study writing, was interrupted much as Mr. Peers
above-mentioned; which minds me of worthy Mr.
Bank's serious Conclusion.

And now I hope you will not think it unbecom-
ing my Character to make this Reflection upon

it, *viz.* that Famines, Pestilences and Earth-
quakes, are joyned by our Blessed Saviour, as
portending future Calamities, and particularly
the Destruction of *Jerusalem* and the Jewish
State; if not the End of the World, St. *Matth.*
24.7. And if, as Philosophers observe, those
gentler Convulsions within the Bowels of the
Earth, which give the Inhabitants but an easie
Jog, do usually portend the Approach of some
more dreadful Earthquake; then surely we have
Reason to fear the worst, because I fear we so
well deserve it, and pray God of his infinite Mercy to avert his future Judgments.

Since my former Account of the Earthquake at *Hull*,
my Cousin *Cookson* has procured to me the following
Account from his Brother, who is a Clergyman near
Lincoln, viz, That he, being about Five in the Evening,
December the 20th past, set with a neighbouring Minister at his House about a Mile from *Navenby*, they
were surpriz'd with a sudden Noise, as if it had been
of two or three Coaches driven furiously down the
Yard, whereupon the Servant was sent to the Door, in
Expectation of some Strangers; but they quickly perceived what it was, by the shaking of the Chairs they
sat upon; they could perceive the very Stones move:
the greatest Damage was to the Gentlewoman of the
House, who was put into such a Fright, that she mis-
carried two Days after. He writes, they were put into
a greater Fright upon the Fastday; when there was so
violent a Storm, they verily thought the Church would
have fallen upon them. We had also at *Leedes* a much
greater Storm the Night preceding the Fast, and a

stronger Wind that Day, than when the fatal Storm was in the South; but a good Providence timed this well, to quicken our too cold Devotions.

Of remarkable Deliverances

As the sad and remarkable Disasters of this Terrible Night were full of a Dismal Variety, so the Goodness of Providence, in the many remarkable Deliverances both by Sea and Land, have their Share in this Account, as they claim an equal Variety and Wonder.

The Sense of extraordinary Deliverances, as it is a Mark of Generous Christianity, so I presume 'tis the best Token, that a good Use is made of the Mercies receiv'd.

The Persons, who desire a thankful Acknowledgment should be made to their Merciful Deliverer, and the Wonders of his Providence remitted to Posterity, shall never have it to say, that the Editor of this Book refus'd to admit so great a Subject a Place in these Memoirs; and therefore, with all imaginable Freedom, he gives the World the Particulars from their own Mouths, and under their own Hands.

The first Account we have from the Reverend Mr. *King*, Lecturer at St. *Martins* in the Fields, as follows.

S I R,

The short Account I now send to shew the Providence of God in the late Dreadful Storm, (if yet it comes not too late) I had from the Mouth of the Gentleman himself, Mr. *Woodgate Gisser* by Name, who is a Neighbour of mine, living in St. *Martin*'s-street in the Parish of St. *Martin*'s in the Fields, and a Sufferer in the common Calamity; is as follows, *viz.*

Between Two and Three of the Clock in the Morning, my Neighbour's Stack of Chimneys fell, and broke down the Roof of my Garret into the Passage going up and down Stairs; upon which, I thought it convenient to retire into the Kitchen with my Family; where we had not been above a Quarter of an Hour, before my Wife sent her Maid to fetch some Necessaries out of a Back Parlour Closer, and as she had shut the Door, and was upon her Return, the very fame Instant my Neighbour's Stack of Chimneys, on the other Side of the House, fell upon my Stack, and beat in the Roof, and so drove down the several Floors through the Parlour into the Kitchen, where the Maid was buried near Five Hours in the Rubbish, without the least Damage or Hurt whatsoever: This her miraculous Preservation was occasion'd (as I afterwards with Surprize found) by her falling into a small Cavity near the Bed, and afterwards (as the declar'd) by her creeping under the Tester that lay hollow by Reason of some Joices that lay athwart each other, which prevented her perishing in the said Rubhish: About Eight in the Morning, when I helped her out of the Ruins, and asked her how he did, and why she did not cry out for Assistance, since she was not (as I suppos'd she had been) dead, and so to let me know he was alive; her Answer was, that truly the for her Part had felt no Hurt, and was not the least affrighted, but lay quiet; and which is more, even flumbred until then.

The Preservation of my self, and the rest of my Family, about Eleven in Number, was, next to the Providence of God, occasion'd by our running into a Vault almost level with the Kitchen upon the Noise and Alarm of the Falling of the Chimeys, which breaking through three Floors, and about two Minutes in passing, gave us the Opportunities of that Retreat. Pray accept of this short Account from

Your Humble Servant, and Lecturer,
James King, M. A.

Feb. 12.
1703.

Another is from a Reverend Minister at - - - - - - - whose Name is to his Letter as follows.

S I R,

I thank you for your charitable Visit not long since; I could have heartily wish'd your Business would have permitted you to have made a little longer Stay at the Parsonage, and then you might have taken a stricker View of the Ruins by the late terrible Wind. Seeing you are pleas'd to desire from the a more particular Account of that fad Disaster I have for your fuller Satisfaction sent you the best I am able to give; and if it be not so perfect, and so exact a one, as you may expect, you may rely upon me it is a true, and a faithful one, and that I do not impose upon you, or the World in the least in any Part of the following Relation. I shall not trouble you with the Uneasiness the Family was under all the fore Part of the Evening, even to a Fault, as I thought, and told them, I did not then apprehend the Wind to be much higher than it had been often on other Times; but went to Bed, hoping we were more afraid than we needed to have been when in Bed, we began to be more sensible of it, and lay most of the Night awake, dreading every Blast till about Four of the Clock in the Morning, when to our thinking it seemed a little to abate; and then we fell asleep, and slept till about Six of the Clock, at which Time my Wife waking, and calling one of her Maids to rise, and come to the Children, the Maid rose; and hasten'd to her; she had not been up above Half an Hour, but all on the sudden we heard a prodigious Noise, as if part of the House had been fallen down: I need not tell you the Consternation we were all in upon this Alarm; in a Minutes Time, I am sure, I was surrounded with all my Infantry, that I thought I should have been overlay'd; I had not even Power to stir one Limb of me, much less to rise, though I could not tell how to lie in Bed. The Shrieks and the Cries of my dear Babes perfectly stun'd me; I think I hear them still in my Ears, I shall not easily, I am confident, if ever, forget them. There I lay preaching Patience to those little Innocent Creatures, till the Day began to appear.

Preces & Lachrima, Prayers and Tears, the Primitive Christians Weapons, we had great Plenty of to defend us withal; but had the House all fallen upon our Heads, we were in that Fright as we could scarce have had Power to rise for the present, or do any thing for our Security. Upon our rising, and sending a Servant to view what she could discover, we soon understood that the Chimney was fallen down, and that with its Fall it had beaten down a great part of that End of the House, *viz.* the Upper Chamber, and the Room under it, which was the Room I chose for my Study: The Chimney was thought as strong, and as well built as most in the Neighbourhood; and it surpriz'd the Mason (whom I immediately sent for to view it) to see it down: but that which was most surprizing to me, was the Manner of its Falling; had it fallen almost any other Way than that it did, it must in all Likelihood have killed the much greater part of my Family, for no less than Nine of us lay at that End of the House, my Wife and Self, and Five Children, and Two Servants, a Maid, and a Man then in my Pay, and so a Servant, though not by the Year: The Bed my Eldest Daughter and the Maid lay in joyned as near as possible to the Chimney, and it was within a very few Yards of the Bed that we lay in; so that as *David* said to *Jonathan*, there seem'd to be but one single Step between Death and us, to all outward Appearance. One Thing I cannot omit, which was very remarkable and surprizing: It pleased God so to order it, that in the Fall of the House two great Spars seem'd to fall so as to pitch themselves on an End, and by that Means to support that other Part of the House which adjoined to the Upper Chamber; or else in all Likelihood, that must also have fallen too at the same Time. The Carpenter (whom we sent for forthwith) when he came, ask'd who plac'd those two Supporters, supposing somebody had been there before him; and when he was told, those two Spars in the Fall so plac'd themselves, he could scarce believe it possible; it was done so artificially, that he declar'd, they scarce needed to have been removed.

In short, Sir, it is impossible to describe the Danger we were in; you your self was an Eyewitness of some Part of what is here related; and I once more assure you, the whole Account I have here given you is true, and what can be attested by the whole Family. None of all those unfortunate Persons who are said to have been killed with the Fall of a Chimney, could well be much more expos'd to Danger than we were; it is owing wholly to that watchful Providence to whom we all are indebted for every Minute of our Lives, that any of us escaped; none but he who never sleeps nor slumbers could have secured us. I beseech Almighty God to give us All that due Sense as we ought to have of so great and so general Calamity; that we truly repent us of those Sins that have so long provoked his Wrath against us, and brought down so heavy a Judgment as this upon us. O that we were so wife as to consider it, and to *sin no more lest a worse thing come upon us!* That it may have this happy Effect upon all the sinful Inhabitants of this Land is, and shall be, the Dayly Prayer of Dear Sir,

Your real Friend and Servant,
John Gipps.

Another Account from a Reverend Minister in *Dorsetshire*, take as follows, *viz.*

S I R,

As you have desired an Account of the Disasters occasion'd by the late Tempest, (which I can assure you was in these Parts very Terrible) so I think my self oblig'd to let you know, that there was a great Mixture of Mercy with it: For though the Hurricane was frightful, and very mischievous, yet God's gracious Providence was therein very remarkable, in retraining its Violence from an universal Destruction: for then there was a Commotion of the Elements of Air, Earth and Water, which then seemed to outvie each other in Mischief; for (in *David*'s Expression, 2 Sam. 22.8.) *The Earth trembled and quak'd, the Foundations of the Heavens moo'd and shook, because God was angry*: and yet, when all was given over for lost, we found our selves more scar'd than hurt; for our Lives was given us for a Prey, and the Tempest did us only so much Damage, as to make us sensible that it might have done us a great deal more, had it not been rebuk'd by the God of Mercy; the Care of whose Providence has been visibly seen in our wonderful Preservations. My Self and Three more of this Parish were then strangely rescued from the Grave: I narrowly escaped with my Life, where I apprehended nothing of Danger; for going out about Midnight to give Orders to my Servants to secure the House, and Reeks of Corn and Furses from being blown all away; as soon as I mov'd out of the Place were I stood, I heard something of a great Weight fall close behind me, and a little after going out with a Light, to fee what it was, I found it to be the great Stone which covered the Top of my Chimney to keep out the Wet; it was almost a Yard square, and very thick, weighing about an Hundred and Fifty Pound. It was blown about a Yard off from the Chimney, and fell Edge-long, and cut the Earth, about four Inches deep, exactly between my Foot-steps; and a little after, whilst sitting under the Clavel of my Kitchen

Chimney, and reaching out my Arm for some Fewel to mend the Fire, I was again strangely preserved from being knock'd on the Head by a Stone of great Weight; it being about a Foot long, Half a Foot broad, and two Inches thick: for as soon as I had drawn in my Arm, I felt something brush against my Elbow, and presently I heard the Stone fall close by my Foot, a third Part of which was broken off by the Violence of the Fall, and skarr'd my Ancle, but did not break the Skin; it had certainly killed me, had it fallen while my Arm was extended. The Top of my Wheat Rick was blown off, and some of the Sheaves were carried a Stones Cast, and with that Violence, that one of them, at that Distance, struck down one *Daniel Fookes* a late Servant of the Lady *Napier*, and so forceably, that he was taken up dead, and to all Appearance remain'd so a great while; but at last was happily recover'd to Life again. His Mother, poor Widow, was at the fame time more fatally threatned at Home, and her Bed had certainly prov'd her Grave, had not the first Noise awaken'd and fear'd her out of Bed; and she was scarce gotten to the Door, when the House fell all in: The Smith's Wife likewise being scar'd at such a Rate, leapt out of Bed, with the little Child in her Arms, and ran hastily out of Doors naked, without Hose or Shooes, to a Neighbour's House; and by that hasty Flight, both their Lives were wonderfully preserved. The Sheets of Lead on *Lytton* Church, were rolled up like Sheets of Parchment, and blown off to a great Distance. At *Strode*, a large Apple Tree, being about a Foot in Square, was broken off cleverly like a Stick, about four Foot from the Root, and carried over an Hedge about ten Foot high; and cast, as if darted, (with the Trunk forward) above fourteen Yards off. And I am credibly inform'd, that at *Ellwood* in the Parish of *Abbotsbury*, a large Wheat Rick (belonging to one *Jolyffe*) was cleverly blown, with its Staddle, off from the Stones, and set down on the Ground in very good Order. I would fain know of the Atheist what mov'd his *Omnipotent Matter* to do such Mischief, &c.

> SIR, *I am*,
>> Your Affectionate Friend and Servant,
>>> though unknown,
>>>> Jacob Cole, *Rect*. of Swyre
>>>>> in County of *Dorset*.

This Account is very remarkable, and well attested, and the Editor of this Collection can vouch to the Reputation of the Relators, tho' not to the Particulars of the Story.

A great Preservation in the late Storm,

bout Three of the Clock in the Morning, the Violence of the Wind blew down a Stack of Chimneys belonging to the dwelling House of Dr. *Gideon Harvey*, (situate in St. *Martin*'s Lane over against the Street End) on the back Part of the next House, wherein dwells Mr. *Robert Richards* an Apothecary, at the Sign of the Unicorn; and Capt. *Theodore Collier* and his Family lodges in the fame. The Chimney fell with that Force as made them pierce thro' the Roofs and all the Floors, carrrying them down quite to the Ground. The two Families, consisting of Fourteen, Men, Women, and Children, besides Three that came in from the next House, were at that Instant dispos'd of as follows, a Footman that us'd to lie in the back Garret, had not a Quarter of an Hour before remov'd himself into the fore Garret, by which means he escap'd the Danger: In the Room under that lay Capt. *Collier*'s Child, of Two Months old, in Bed with the Nurse, and a Servant Maid lay on the Bed by her; the Nurse's Child lying in a Cribb by the Bedside, which was found, with the Child safe in it, in the Kitchen, where the Nurse and Maid likewise found themselves; their Bed being shatter'd in Pieces, and they a little bruis'd by falling down Three Stories: Capt. *Collier*'s Child was in about Two Hours found unhurt in some Pieces of the Bed and Curtains, which had fallen through Two Floors only, and hung on some broken Rafters in that Place, which was the Parlour: In the Room under This, being one Pair of Stairs from the Strand two from the Kitchen, was Capt. *Collier* in his Bed, and his Wife just by the Bed side, and her Maid a little behind her, who likewise found her self in the Kitchin a little bruis'd, and ran out to cry for Help for her Master and Mistress, who lay buried under the Ruins: Mrs. *Collier* was, by the timely Aid of Neighbours who remov'd the Rubbish from her, taken out in about Half an Hours Time, having receiv'd no Hurt but the Fright, and an Arm a little bruis'd: Capt. *Collier* in about Halsan Hour more was likewise taken out unhurt. In the Parlour were sitting Mr. *Richards* with his Wife, the Three Neighbours, and the rest of his Family, a little Boy of about a Year old lying in the Cradle, they all run out at the first Noise, and escap'd; Mrs. *Richards* staying a little longer than the rest, to pull the Cradle with her Child in it along with her, but the House fell too suddenly on it, and buried the Child under the Ruins, a Rafter fell on her Foot. and bruis'd it a little, at which she likewise made her Escape, and brought in the Neighbours, who soon uncovered the Head of the Cradle, and cutting it off, took the Child out alive and well. This wonderful Preservation being worthy to be transmitted to Posterity, we do attest to be true in every Particular. Witness our Hands,

> *Gideon Harvey.*
> *Theo. Collier.*
> *Robert Richards.*

London,
Nov. 27. 1703.

These Accounts of like Nature are particularly attested by Persons of known Reputation and Integrity.

S I R ,

n order to promote the good Design of your Book, in perpetuating the Memory of God's signal Judgment on this Nation, by the late dreadful Tempest of Wind, which has hurl'd so many Souls into Eternity; and likewise his Providence in the miraculous Preservation of several Persons Lives, who were expos'd to the utmost Hazards in that Hurricane: I shall here give you a short but true Instance of the latter, which several Persons can witness besides my self; and if you think proper may insert the same in the Book you design for that Purpose; which is as follows. At the *Saracen*'s Head in *Friday* Street, a Country Lad lodging three Pair of Stairs next the Roof of the House, was wonderfully preserv'd from Death; for about Two a Clock that *Saturday* Morning the 27th of *November*, (which prov'd fatal to so many) there fell a Chimney upon the Roof, under which he lay, and bear it down through the Ceiling (the Weight of the Tiles, Bricks, &c. being judged by a Workman to be about Five Hundred Weight) into the Room, fell exactly between the Beds Feet and Door of the Room, which are not Two Yards distance from each other, it being but small: the sudden Noise awaking the Lad, he jumps out of Bed endeavouring to find the Door, but was stopt by the great Dust and falling of more Bricks, &c. and finding himself prevented, in this Fear he got into Bed again, and remain'd there till the Day Light, (the Bricks and Tiles still falling between-whiles about his Bed) and then got up without any Hurt, or so much as a Tile or Brick falling on the Bed; the only thing he complain'd of to me, was his being almost choak'd with Dust when he got out of Bed, or put his Head out from under the Cloaths: There was a great Weight of Tiles and Bricks, which did not break through, as the Workmen inform me, just over the Beds Tester, enough to have crush'd him to Death, if they had fallen: Thus he lay safe among the Dangers that threatned him, whilst wakeful Providence preserv'd him. And SIR, if this be worthy your taking Notice of, I am ready to justify the same. In Witness whereof, here is my Name,

Henry Mayers

Dec. 3. 1703.

A great Preservation in the late Storm.

illiam Phelps and Frances his Wife, living at the Corner of *Old Southampton Buildings*, over against *Gray's-Inn Gate* in *Holborn*, they lying up three pair of Stairs, in the Backroom, that was only lath'd and plaister'd, he being then very ill, he was fored to lie in a Table-Bed in the same Room: about One a Clock in the Morning, on the 27th of *November* last, the Wind blew down a Stack of Chimneys of seven Funnels that stood very high; which broke through the Roof,

and fell into the Room, on her Bed; so that the
was buried a live, as one may say: The crying out,
Mr. Phelps, *Mr.* Phelps, *the House is fall'n upon
me*, there being so much on her that one could but
just hear her speak; a Coachman and a Footman
lying on the fame Floor, I soon call'd them to my
Assistance. We all fell to work, tho' we flood in the
greatest Danger; and through the Goodness of God
we did take her out, without the least hurt; neither
was any of us hurt, tho' there was much fell after
we took her out. And when we took the Bricks off
the Bed the next Morning, we found the Frame of
the Bed on Which the lay broke all to pieces,

William Phelps.

Another great Preservation

r. *John Hanson*, Register of *Eaton College*,
being at *London* about his Affairs, and lying that dreadful Night, Nov. 26, at the
Bell-Savage Inn on *Ludgate Hill*, was, by the Fall
of a Stack of Chimneys (which broke through the
Roof, and beat down two Floors above him, and
also that in which he lay) carried in his Bed down
to the Ground, without the least hurt, his Cloaths,
and every thing besides in the Room, being buried
in the Rubbish; it having pleased God so to order
it, that just so much of the Floor and Ceiling of the
Room (from which he fell) as covered his Bed, was

not broken down. Of this great Mercy he prays he may live for ever mindful, and be for ever thankful to Almighty God.

S I R,

The Design of your Collecting the remarkable Accidents of the late Storm coming to my Hands, I thought my self obliged to take this Opportunity of making a publick Acknowledgment of the wonderful Providence of Heaven to me, namely, the Preservation of my only Child from imminent Danger.

Two large Stacks of Chimneys, containing each five Funnels, beat through the Roof, in upon the Bed where the lay, without doing her the least Harm, the Servant who lay with her being very much bruised. There were several Loads of Rubbish upon the Bed before my Child was taken out of it.

This extraordinary Deliverance I desire always thankfully to remember. I was so nearly touch'd by this Accident, that I could not take so much notice as I intended of this Storm; yet I observ'd the Wind gradually to encrease from One a Clock till a Quarter after Five, or thereabouts: at which time it seem'd to be at the highest; when every Gust did not only return with greater Celerity, but also with more Force.

From about a Quarter before Six it sensibly decreas'd. I went often to the Door, at which times I observ'd, that every Gust was preceded by small

Flashes, which, to my Observation, did not dart perpendicularly, but seem'd rather to skim along the Surface of the Ground; nor did they appear to be of the same kind with the common Light'ning Flashes.

I must confess I cannot help thinking that the Earth it self suffer'd some Convulsion; and that for this Reason, because several Springs, for the space of 48 Hours afterwards, were very muddy, which were never known to be so by any Storm of Wind or Rain before: nor indeed is it possible, they lying so low, could be affected by any thing less than a Concussion of the Earth it self.

How far these small Hints may be of use to the more ingenious Enquirers into this matter, I shall humbly leave to their Consideration, and subscribe my self,

SIR,

Your humble Servant,
Joseph Clench,
Apothecary in Jermyn *Street,*
near St. James's.

Dec. 8. 1703.

S I R,

This comes to let you know that I received yours in the *Downs*, for which I thank you. I expected to have seen you in *London* before now, had we not met with a most violent Storm in our way to *Chatham*. On the 27th of the last Month, about Three of the Clock in the Morning, we lost all our Anchors and drove to Sea: about Six we lost our Rother, and were left in a most deplorable condition to the merciless Rage of the Wind and Seas: we also sprung a Leak, and drove 48 Hours expecting to perish. But it pleased God to give us a wonderful Deliverance, scarce to be parallell'd in History; for about Midnight we were drove into foul Water, and soon after our Ship struck upon the Sands: the Sea broke over us, we expected every minute that she would drop to pieces, and that we should all be swallowed up in the Deep; but in less than two hours time we drove over the Sands, and got (without Rother or Pilot, or any Help but Almighty God's) into this Place, where we run our Ship on shore, in order to save our Lives: but it has pleased God also, far beyond our expectation, to save our Ship, and bring us safe off again last Night. We shall remain here a considerable while to refit our Ship, and get a new Rother. Our Deliverance is most remarkable, that in the middle of a dark Night we should drive over a Sand where a Ship that was not half our Bigness durst not venture to come in the Day; and then, without knowing where we were, drive into a narrow place where we have saved both Lives and Ship. I pray God give us all Grace to be thankful, and never forget so great a mercy, I am,

Your affectionate Friend and humble Servant,

Henry Barclay.

Russel, as Helversluce in Holland, Dec. 16. 1793.

S I R,

According to the publick I send you two or three Observations of mine upon the late dreadful Tempest: As, 1. In the Parish of St. Mary Cray, Kent, a poor Man, with his Wife and Child, were but just gone out of their Bed, when the Head of their House fell in upon it; which must have kill'd them.

2. A great long Stable in the Town, near the Church, was blown off the Foundation entirely at one sudden Blast, from the West side to the East, and cast out into the High-way, over the Heads of five Horses, and a Carter feeding them at the same time, and not one of them hurt, nor the Rack or Manger touch'd, which are yet standing to the Admiration of all Beholders.

3. As the Church at *Heyes* received great Damage, so the Spire, with one Bell in it, were blown away over the Church-yard.

4. The Minister of *South Ash* had a great Deliverance from a Chimney falling in upon his Bed just as he rose, and hurt only his Feet; as blessed be God, our Lives have been all very miraculously preserv'd, tho' our Buildings every where damag'd. You may depend on all, as certify'd by me,

Thomas Watts,
Vicar of and St. Mary Cray.

There are an innumerable variety of Deliverances, besides these, which deserve a Memorial to future Ages; but these are noted from the Letters, and at the Request of the Persons particularly concern'd.

Particularly, 'tis a most remarkable Story of a Man belonging to the Mary, a fourth Rate Man of War, lost upon the Goodwin Sands; and all the Ship's Company but himself being lost, he, by the help of a piece of the broken Ship, got a-board the *Northumberland*; but the Violence of the Storm continuing, the *Northumberland* ran the same fate with the Mary, and coming on shore upon the same Sand, was split to pieces by the Violence of the Sea: and yet this Person, by a singular Providence, was one of the 64 that were delivered by a Deal Hooker out of that Ship, all the rest perishing in the Sea.

A poor Sailor of *Brighthelmston* was taken up after he had hung by his Hands and Feet on the top of a Mast 48 hours, the Sea raging so high, that no Boat durst go near him.

A Hoy run on shore on the Rocks in *Milford Haven*, and just splitting to pieces (as by Captain *Soam*'s Letter) a Boar drove by, being broke from another Vessel, with no body in it, and came so near the Vessel, as that two Men jumpt into it, and sav'd their Lives: the Boy could not jump so far, and was drowned.

Five Sailors shifted three Vessels on an Island near the *Humber*, and were at last sav'd by a Long-boat out of the fourth.

A Waterman in the River of *Thames* lying asleep in the Cabbin of a Barge, at or near *Black-Fryers*, was driven thro' Bridge in the Storm, and the Barge went of her self into the Tower-Dock, and lay safe on shore; the Man never wak'd, nor heard the Storm, till 'twas Day; and, to his great Astonishment, he found himself safe as above.

Two Boys in the Poultry lodging in a Garret or Upper- room, were, by the Fall of Chimneys, which broke thro' the Floors, carried quite to the bottom of the Cellar, and receiv'd no Damage at all.

S I R,

At my Return home on Saturday at Night, I receiv'd yours: and having said nothing in my last concerning the Storm, I send this to 'tell you, that I hear of nothing done by it in this Country that may seem to deserve a particular Remark. Several Houses and Barns were stript of their Thatch, some Chimneys and Gables blown down, and several Stacks of Corn and Hay very much dispers'd; but I hear not of any Persons either kill'd or maim'd. A Neighbour of ours was upon the Ridge of his Barn endeavouring to secure the Thatch, and the Barn at that instant was overturn'd by the Storm; but by the good Providence of God, the Man received little or no harm. I say no more, not knowing of any thing more remarkable. I am sorry that other Places were such great Sufferers, and I pray God avert the like Judgments for the future. I am

Your real Friend to serve you,
Hen. Marshal.

Orby, Jan. 18.
1703.

S I R,

I have no particular Relation to make to you of any Deliverance in the late Storm, more than was common with me to all the rest that were in it: but having, to divert melancholly Thoughts while it lasted, turn'd into Verse the CXLVIII Psalm to the 9th, and afterwards all the Psalm; I give you leave to publish it with the rest of those Memoirs on that Occasion you are preparing for the Press.

SIR, *Your*, & c.
Henry Squier.

I. Verse 1, 2.

*Allelujah: From Heav'n
The tuneful Praise begin;
Let Praise to God be giv'n
Beyond the Starry Scene:
Ye Angels sing
His joyful Praise;
Your Voices raise
Ye swift of Wing.*

II. 3,4.

*Praise him, thou radiant Sun,
The Spring of all thy Light;
Praise him thou changing Moon,
And all the Stars of Night:
Ye Hearns declare
His glorious Fame;
And waves that swim
Above the Sphere.*

III. 5, 6.

Let all his Praises sing,
>> His Goodness and his Power,
For at his Call they spring,
>> And by his Grace endure;
>>> That joins 'em fast,
>>>> The Chain is fram'd,
>>>> Their Bounds are nam'd,
>> And never past.

IV. 7, 8.

Thou Earth his Praise proclaim,
>> Devouring Gulfs and Deeps;
Ye Fires, and fire-like Flame,
>> That o'er the Meadows sweeps;
>>> Thou rattling Hail,
>>>> And flaky Snow,
>>>> And Winds that blow
>> To do his Will.

V. 9, 10.

Ye Prodigies of Earth
>> And Hills of lesser size,
Cedars of nobler Birth,
>> And all ye fruitful Trees;
>>> His Praises Show
>>>> All things that move,
>>>> That fly above,

Or creep below.

VI. 11, 12.

Monarchs, and ye their Praise,
The num'rous Multitude;
Ye Judges, Triumphs raise;
And all of nobler Blood:
Of every kind,
And ev'ry Age,
Your Hearts engage,
In Praises join'd.

VII. 13, 14:

Let all his glorious Name
Unite to celebrate;
Above the Heaven's his Fame;
His Fame that's only great:
His Peoples Stay
And Praise is He,
And e're will be:
Hallelujah.

The two following Letters, coming from Persons in as great Danger as any could be, are plac'd here, as proper to be call'd' Deliverances of the greatest and strangest kind.

From on board a Ship blown out of the Downs *to* Norway.

S I R,

I cannot but write to you of the Particulars of our sad and terrible Voyage to this Place. You know we were, by my last, riding safe in the Downs, waiting a fair Wind, to make the best of our way to *Portsmouth*, and there to expect the *Lisbon* Convoy.

We had had two terrible Storms, one on the *Friday* before, and one on *Thursday*; the one the 18th, the other the 25th of *November*: In the last I expected we shou'd have founder'd at an Anchor; for our Ground Tackle being new and very good held us fast, but the Sea broke upon us so heavy and quick, that we were in danger two or three times of Foundring as we rod: but, as it pleas'd God we rid it out, we began to think all was over, and the Bitterness of Death was past.

There was a great Fleet with us in the *Downs*, and several of them were driven from their Anchors, and made the best of their way out to Sea for fear of going on shore upon the *Goodwin*. the Grand Fleet was just come in from the *Streights*, under Sir *Cloudsly Shovel*; and the Great Ships being design'd for the River, lay to Leeward: Most of the Ships that went out in the Night appeard in the Morning; and I think there was none known to be lost, but one Dutch Vessel upon the *Goodwin*.

But the next Day, being *Friday*, in the Evening, it began to gather to Windward; and as it had blown very hard all Day, at Night the Wind freshen'd, and we all expected a stormy Night. We saw the Men of War struck their Top-masts, and rode with two Cables an-end: so we made all as snug as we could, and prepar'd for the worst.

In this condition we rid it out till about 12 a-clock; when, the Fury of the Wind encreating, we began to see Destruction before us: the Objects were very dreadful on every side; and tho' it was very dark, we had Light enough to fee our own Danger, and the Danger of those near us. About One a-clock the Ships began to drive, and we saw several come by us without a Mast standing, and in the utmost Distress.

By Two-a-clock we could hear Guns firing in several Parts of this Road, as Signals of Distress; and tho' the Noise was very great with the Sea and Wind, yet we could distinguish plainly, in some short Intervals, the Cries of poor Souls in Extremities.

By Four-a-clock we miss'd the *Mary* and the *Northumberland*, who rid not far from us, and found they were driven from their Anchors; but what became of them, God knows and soon after a large Man of War came driving down upon us, all her Masts gone, and in a dreadful Condition. We were in the utmost Despair at this fight, for we saw no avoiding her coming thwart *our Haiser*: she drove at last so near us, that I was just gowing to order the Mate to cut away, when it pleas'd God the Ship sheer'd contrary to our Expectation to Windward, and the Man of War, which we found to be the *Sterling Castle*, drove clear off us, not two Ships Lengths to Leeward.

It was a Sight full of terrible Particulars, to see a Ship of Eighty Guns and about Six Hundred Men in that dismal Case; she had cut a way all her Masts, the Men were all in the Confusions of Death and Despair; she had neither Anchor, nor Cable, nor Boat to help her; the Sea breaking over her in a terrible Manner, that sometimes the seem'd all under Water; and they knew, as well as we that saw her, that they drove by the Tempest directly for the Goodwin, where they could expect nothing but Destruction: The Cries of the Men, and the firing their Guns, One by One, every Half Minute for Help, terrified us in such a Manner, that I think we were half dead with the Horror of it.

All this while we rid with two Anchors a-head, and in great Distress: To fire Guns for Help, I saw was to no Purpose, for if any Help was to be had, there were so many other Objects for it, that we could not expect it, and the Storm still encreasing.

Two Ships, a-head of us, had rid it out till now, which was towards Five in the Morning, when they both drove from their Anchors, and one of them coming foul of a small Pink, they both sunk together; the other drove by us, and having one Malt standing, I think it was her Main Mast, she attempted to spread a little Peak of her Sail, and so stood away before it; I suppose she went away to Sea.

At this time, the Raging of the Sea was so violent, and the Tempest doubled its Fury in such a Manner, that my Mate told me, we had better go away to Sea, for 'twould be impossible to ride it out; I was not of his Opinion, but was for cutting my Masts by the Board, which at last we did, and parted with them with as little Damage as could be expected, and we thought the rid easier for it by a great deal; and I believe, had it blown two Hours longer, we should have rid it out, having two new Cables out, and our best Bower and Sheet Anchor down: But about Half an Hour after Five to Six, it blew, if it be possible to conceive it so, as hard again as it had done before, and first our best Bower Anchor came Home, the Mate, who felt it give way, cried out, we are all undone, for the Ship drove; I found it too true, and, upon as short a Consultation as the Time would admit, we concluded to put out to Sea before we were driven too far to Leward, when it would be impossible to avoid the Goodwin.

So we slipt our Sheet Cable, and sheering the Ship towards the Shore, got her Head about, and food away afore it; Sail we had none, nor Mast standing: Our Mate had set up a Jury Missen but no Canvass could bear the Fury of the Wind, yet he fasten'd an old Tarpaulin so as that it did the Office of a Missen and kept us from driving too fast to Leeward.

In this Condition we drove out of the *Downs*, and past so near the *Goodwin*, that we could see several great Ships fast a ground, and beating to Pieces. We drove in this desperate Condition till Day-break, without any Abatement of the Storm, and our Men heartless and dispirited, tir'd with the Service of the Night, and every Minute expecting Death.

About 8 a-Clock, my Mate told me, he perceiv'd the Wind to abate; but it blew still such a Storm, that if we had not had a very tite Ship, she must have founder'd, as we were now farther off at Sea, and by my Guess might be in the mid Way between *Harwich* and the *Brill*, the Sea we found run longer, and did not break so quick upon us as before, but it ran exceeding high, and we having no Sail to keep us to rights, we lay wallowing in the Trough of the Sea in a miserable Condition: We saw several Ships in the same Condition with our selves, but could neither help them, nor they us; and one we saw founder before our Eyes, and all the People perish'd.

Another dismal Object we met with, which was an open Boat full of Men, who, as we may suppose, had lost their Ship; any Man may suppose, what Condition a Boat must be in, if we were in so bad a Case in a good Ship: we were soon tost out of their Sight, and what became of them any one may guess; if they had been within Cables Length of us we could not have help'd them.

About Two a Clock in the Afternoon, the Wind encreased again, and we made no doubt it would prove as bad a Night as before; but that Gust held not above Half an Hour.

All Night it blew exceffive hard, and the next Day, which was Sabbath Day, about Eleven a Clock it abated, but still blew hard: about three it blew something moderately, compar'd with the former; and we got up a Jury-Main-Mast, and rigg'd it as well as we could, and with a Main Sail lower'd almost to the Deck, stood at a great Rate afore it all Night and the next Day, and on Tuesday Morning we saw Land, but could not tell where it was; but being not in a Condion to keep the Sea, we run in, and made Signals of Distress; some Pilots came off to us, by whom we were inform'd we had reached the Coast of Norway, and having neither Anchor nor Cable on board capable to ride the Ship, a Norwegian Pilot came on board, and brought us into a Creek where we had smooth Water, and lay by till we got Help, Cables, and Anchors, by which means we are safe in Place.

Your Humble Servant,
J. Adams.

From onboard the John and Mary, *riding in* Yarmouth Roads *during the great Storm, but now in the River of* Thames.

S I R,

earing of your good Design of preserving the for the Benefit of Posterity, I cannot let you want the Particulars as happen'd to us on board our Ship.

We came over the Bar of *Tinmouth* about the
having had terrible blowing Weath-
er for almost a Week, insomuch that we were
twice driven back almost the Length of *Newcastle*, with much Difficulty and Danger we got well
over that, and made the High-land about *Cromer*
on the North-side of *Norfolk* here it blew so hard
the *Wednesday* Night before, that we could not
keep the Sea, nor fetch the Roads of *Yarmouth* but
as the Coast of *Norfolk* was a Weather-shore, we
hall'd as close *Cromer* as we durst lie, the Shore
there being very flat; here we rode *Wednesday* and
Thursday, the 24th and 25th of *November*.

We could not reckon our selves safe here, for as
this is the most dangerous Place between *London*
and *Newcastle*, and has been particularly fatal to
our Colliers, so we were very uneasy: I considered
that when such Tempestuous Weather happen'd,
as this seem'd to threaten, nothing is more frequent than for the Wind to shift Points; and if it
should have blown half the Wind from the South
East, as now blew from the South West, we must
have gone a-shore there, and been all lost for being
embayed; there we should have had no putting out
to Sea, nor staying there.

This Consideration made me resolve to begon,
and thinking on Friday Morning the Wind slack-
end a little, I weigh'd and stood away for *Yarmouth*
Roads; and with great Boating and Labour got into
the Roads about One in the Afternoon, being a little after Flood, we found a very great Fleet in the

Roads; there was above Three Hundred Sail of Colliers, not reckoning above Thirty Sail which I left behind me, that rode it out thereabouts, and there was a great Fleet just come from *Russia*, under the Convoy of the Reserve Frigate, and Two other Men of War; and about a Hundred Sail of Coasters, Hall Men, and such small Craft.

We had not got to an Anchor, moor'd, and set all to Rights, but I found the Wind freshen'd, the Clouds gather'd, and all look'd very black to Windward; and my Mate told me, he wish'd he had staid where we were, for he would warrant it we had a blowing Night of it.

We did what we could to prepare for it, struck our Top-mast, and flung our Yards, made all tite and fast upon Deck; the Night prov'd very dark, and the Wind blew a Storm about Eight a Clock, and held till Ten, when we thought it abated a little, but at Eleven it freshen'd again, and blew very hard; we rid it out very well till Twelve, when we veer'd out more Cable, and in about Half an Hour after, the Wind encreasing, let go our Sheet Anchor by One a Clock it blew a dreadful Storm, and though our Anchors held very well, the Sea came over us in such a vast Quantity, that we was every Hour in Danger of Foundring: About Two a Clock the Sea fill'd our Boat as the lay upon the Deck, and we was glad to let her go over board for Fear of staving in our Decks: Our Mate would then have cut our Mast by the Board, but I was not willing, and told him, I thought we had better flip our Cables, and go out to Sea, he argued she was a deep Ship, and would not live in the Sea, and was very eager for cutting away the Mast; but I was loth to part with my Mast, and could not tell where to run for Shelter if I lost them.

About Three a Clock abundance of Ships drove away, and came by us; some with all their Masts gone, and foul of one another; in a sad Condition my Men said they saw Two founder'd together, but I was in the Cabin, and cannot fay I saw it. I saw a Russia Ship come foul of a Collier, and both drove away together out of our Sight, but I am told since the Russia Man funk by her Side.

In this Condition we rid till about Three a Clock, the Russia Ships which lay a-head of me, and the Men of War, who lay a-head of them, fir'd their Guns for Help, but 'twas in vain to expect it; the Sea went too high for any Boat to live. About Five, the Wind blew at that prodigious Rate, that there was no Possibility of riding it out, and all the Ships in the Road seem'd to us to drive: Yet still our Anchors held it, and I began to think we should ride it out there, or founder; when a Ship's long Boat came driving against us, and gave such a Shock on the Bow that I thought it must have been a Ship come foul of us, and expected to sink all at once; our Men said there was some People in the Boat, but as the Sea went so high no Man durst stand upon the Fore-castle, so no Body could be sure of it; the Boat stav'd to pieces with the Blow, and went away, some on One Side of us and some on the other; but whether our Cable receiv'd any Damage by it or not we cannot tell, but our Sheet Cable gave Way immediately, and as the other was not able to hold us alone, we immediately drove; we had then no more to do, but to put afore the Wind, which we did: it pleased God by this Time the Tide of Ebb was begun, which something abated the Height of the Sea, but still it went exceeding high; we saw a great many Ships in the same Condition with our selves, and expecting every Moment to sink in the Sea. In this Extremity we drove till Daylight when we found the Wind abated, and we stood in for the Shore, and coming under the Lee of the Cliff near *Scarbro*, we got so much Shelter, as that our small Bower Anchors would ride us.

I can give you no Account but this; but sure such a Tempest never was in the World. They say here, that of Eighty Sail in *Grimsby Road*, they can hear of but Sixteen; yet the rest are all blown away, Here is about Twelve or Fourteen Sail of Ships come in to this Place, and more are standing in for the Shore.

Yours, &c.

Abundance of other strange Deliverances have been related, but with so small Authority as we dare not convey them into the World under the same Character with the rest; and have therefore chose to omit them.

The CONCLUSION

he Editor of this Book has labour'd under some Difficulties in this Account and one of the chief has been, how to avoid too many Particulars, the Crowds of Relations which he has been obliged to lay by to bring the Story into a Compass tolerable to the Reader. And tho' some of the Letters inserted are written in a homely Stile, and exprest after the Country Fashion from whence they came, the Author chose to make them speak their own Language, rather than by dressing them in other Words make the Authors forget they were their own. We receiv'd a Letter, very particular, relating to the Bishop of *Bath* and *Wells*, and reflecting upon his Lordship for some Words he spoke, That he had rather have his Brains knock'd out, than &c. relating to his Inferiour Clergy. The Gentleman takes the Disaster for a Judgment of God on him: But as in his Letter the Person owns himself the Bishop's Enemy, fills his Letter with some Reflexions indecent, at least for us and at last, tho' he dates from *Samerton*, yet baulks setting his Name to his Letter: for these Reasons we could not satisfie to record the Matter, and leave a Charge on the Name of that unfortunate Gentleman, which, he being dead, could not answer, and we alive could not prove. And on these Accounts hope the Reverend Gentleman who sent the Letter will excuse Us.

Also we have omitted, tho' our List of Particulars promis'd such a thing, An Account of some unthinking Wretches, who pass'd over this dreadful Judgment with Banter, Scoffing, and Contempt. 'Tis a Subject ungrateful to recite, and full of Horror to read; and we had much rather cover such Actions with a general Blank in Charity to the Offenders, and in hopes of their Amendment.

One unhappy Accident I cannot omit, and which is brought us from good Hands, and happen'd in a Ship homeward bound from the West-Indies. The Ship was in the utmost Danger of Foundring; and when the Master saw all, as he thought, lost, his Masts gone, the Ship leaky, and expecting her every moment to sink under him, fill'd with Despair, he calls to him the Surgeon of the Ship, and by a fatal Contract, as soon made as hastily executed, they resolv'd to prevent the Death they fear'd by one more certain; and going into the Cabbin, they both shot themselves with their Pistols. It pleas'd God the Ship recover'd the Distress, was driven safe into and the Captain just liv'd to see the desperate Course he took might have been spar'd; the Surgeon died immediately.

There are several very remarkable Cases come to our Hands since the finishing this Book, and several have been promis'd which are not come in; and the Book having been so long promis'd, and so earnestly desir'd by several Gentlemen

that have already assisted that way, the Undertakers could not prevail with themselves to delay
it any longer.

F I N I S

Index

G

H

Y